IS-100.B: Introduction to Incident Command System, ICS-100

By

Fema

10/21/2013

Lesson Summary

Lesson 1: Course Welcome & ICS Overview

Course Goal

The overall course goal is to promote effective response by:

- Familiarizing you with how Incident Command System (ICS) principles are used to manage incidents.
- Preparing you to coordinate with response partners from all levels of government and the private sector.

IS-100.b follows the National Incident Management System (NIMS) guidelines. To learn more about NIMS, you should complete IS-700.A, National Incident Management System, An Introduction.

Overall Course Objectives

At the completion of this course, you should be familiar with:

- ICS applications.
- ICS organizational principles and elements.
- ICS positions and responsibilities.
- ICS facilities and functions.
- ICS planning.

In addition, you will learn the steps you should take to be accountable for your actions during an incident.

What Is the Incident Command System?

The Incident Command System (ICS) is a standardized approach to incident management that:

- Enables a coordinated response among various jurisdictions and agencies.
- Establishes common processes for planning and managing resources.
- Allows for the integration of facilities, equipment, personnel, procedures, and communications operating within a common organizational structure.

Incident Command System: Helping Us Meet Our Mission

Disaster can strike anytime, anywhere. It takes many forms—a hurricane, an earthquake, a tornado, a flood, a fire or a hazardous spill, or an act of terrorism. An incident can build over days or weeks, or hit suddenly, without warning.

A poorly managed incident response can undermine our safety and well being. With so much at stake, we must effectively manage our response efforts.

Although most incidents are handled locally, partnerships among local, tribal, State, and Federal agencies as well as nongovernmental and private-sector organizations may be required.

As partners, we must respond together in a seamless, coordinated fashion.

The Incident Command System, or ICS, helps ensure integration of our response efforts. ICS is a standardized, on-scene, all-hazards approach to incident management. ICS allows all responders to adopt an integrated organizational structure that matches the complexities and demands of the incident while respecting agency and jurisdictional authorities. Although ICS promotes standardization, it is not without needed flexibility. For example, the ICS organizational structure can expand or contract to meet incident needs.

In this course, you'll learn ICS principles. And more importantly, you'll learn to interface better with your response partners.

Incident Command System Origins

The Incident Command System was developed in the 1970s following a series of catastrophic fires in California. Property damage ran into the millions, and many people died or were injured.

The personnel assigned to determine the causes of these disasters studied the case histories and discovered that response problems could rarely be attributed to lack of resources or failure of tactics.

Homeland Security Presidential Directives

- HSPD-5 identified steps for improved coordination in response to incidents. It requires the Department of Homeland Security (DHS) to coordinate with other Federal departments and agencies and State, local, and tribal governments to establish a National Response Framework (NRF) and a National Incident Management System (NIMS).
- PPD-8 - describes the Nation's approach to preparedness-one that involves the whole community, including individuals, businesses, community- and faith-based organizations, schools, tribes, and all levels of government (Federal, State, local, tribal and territorial).

NIMS and NRF

- NIMS provides a systematic, proactive approach to guide departments and agencies at all levels of government, nongovernmental organizations, and the private sector to work seamlessly to prevent, protect against, respond to, recover from, and mitigate the effects of incidents, regardless of cause, size, location, or complexity, in order to reduce the loss of life and property and harm to the environment.
- The NRF is a guide to how the Nation conducts all-hazards response – from the smallest incident to the largest catastrophe. This key document establishes a comprehensive, national, all-hazards approach to domestic incident response. The Framework identifies the key response principles, roles, and structures that organize national response. It describes how communities, States, the Federal Government, and private-sector and nongovernmental partners apply these principles for a coordinated, effective national response.

NIMS Components

NIMS is much more than just using the Incident Command System or an organization chart.

NIMS is a consistent, nationwide, systematic approach that includes the following components:

- **Preparedness**
  Actions taken to plan, organize, equip, train, and exercise to build and sustain the capabilities necessary to prevent, protect against, mitigate the effects of, respond to, and recover from those threats that pose the greatest risk. Within NIMS, preparedness focuses on the following elements: planning; procedures and protocols; training and exercises; personnel qualifications, licensure, and certification; and equipment certification.
- **Communications and Information Management**
  Emergency management and incident response activities rely on communications and information systems that provide a common operating picture to all command and coordination sites. NIMS describes the requirements necessary for a standardized framework for communications and emphasizes the need for a common operating picture. This component is based on the concepts of interoperability,

reliability, scalability, and portability, as well as the resiliency and redundancy of communications and information systems.

- **Resource Management**
  Resources (such as personnel, equipment, or supplies) are needed to support critical incident objectives. The flow of resources must be fluid and adaptable to the requirements of the incident. NIMS defines standardized mechanisms and establishes the resource management process to identify requirements, order and acquire, mobilize, track and report, recover and demobilize, reimburse, and inventory resources.

- **Command and Management**
  The Command and Management component of NIMS is designed to enable effective and efficient incident management and coordination by providing a flexible, standardized incident management structure. The structure is based on three key organizational constructs: the Incident Command System, Multiagency Coordination Systems, and Public Information.

- **Ongoing Management and Maintenance**
  Within the auspices of Ongoing Management and Maintenance, there are two components: the National Integration Center (NIC) and Supporting Technologies.

The components of NIMS were not designed to stand alone, but to work together.

Command and Management Elements

The NIMS Command and Management component facilitates incident management. This component includes the following elements: Incident Command System, Multiagency Coordination Systems, and Public Information.

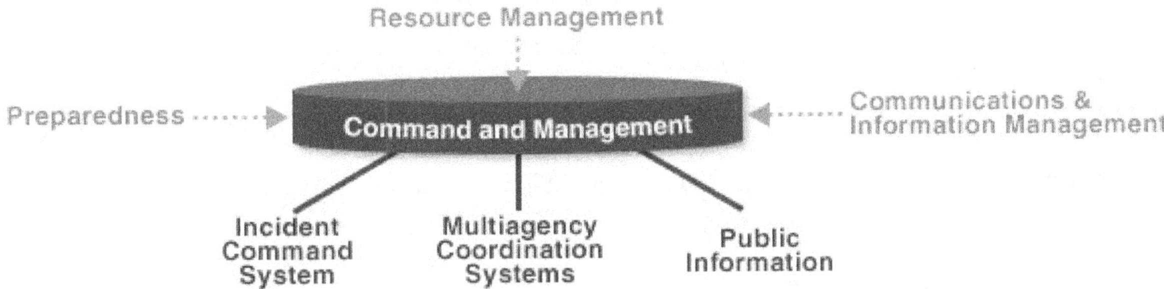

Lessons Learned

After-action reports from ineffective incident responses find that response problems are far more likely to result from inadequate management than from any other single cause. Weaknesses in incident management are often due to:

- Lack of accountability, including unclear chains of command and supervision.
- Poor communication, due to both inefficient uses of available communications systems and conflicting codes and terminology.
- Lack of an orderly, systematic planning process.
- No common, flexible, predesigned management structure that enabled commanders to delegate responsibilities and manage workloads efficiently.
- No predefined methods to integrate interagency requirements into the management structure and planning process effectively.

Using ICS enables us to avoid these weaknesses in all types of incident response.

Without ICS: Confusion and Poor Decisions

Without ICS, incident responses typically:

- Lack accountability, because of unclear chains of command and supervision.
- Have poor communications, due to both inefficient uses of available communications systems and conflicting codes and terminology.
- Use unsystematic planning processes and fail to reach objectives.
- Are unable to efficiently integrate responders into standard organizational structures and roles.

ICS: Built on Best Practices

ICS is based on decades of lessons learned. Using management best practices, ICS helps to ensure:

- The safety of responders, community members, and others.
- The achievement of response objectives.
- The efficient use of resources.

ICS has been tested in more than 30 years of emergency and nonemergency applications, by all levels of government and in nongovernmental and private-sector organizations.

When Is ICS Used?

ICS can be used to manage any type of incident, including a planned event (e.g., the Olympics, Presidential inauguration, etc.). The use of ICS is applicable to all hazards, including:

- **Natural Hazards:** Disasters, such as fires, tornadoes, floods, ice storms, earthquakes, foodborne illnesses, or epidemics.
- **Technological Hazards:** Dam breaks, radiological or hazmat releases, power failures, or medical device defects.
- **Human-Caused Hazards:** Criminal or terrorist acts , school violence, or other civil disturbances.

ICS: Not Just For Large-Scale Incidents

As a system, ICS is extremely useful. Not only does it provide an organizational structure for incident management, but it also guides the process for planning, building, and adapting that structure.

Using ICS for every incident or planned event helps improve and maintain skills needed for the large-scale incidents.

Lesson Summary

You have completed the ICS Overview lesson. This lesson presented the following key points:

- ICS is a standardized management tool that allows better coordination and use of resources.
- ICS represents organizational "best practices," and has become the standard for emergency management.
- ICS can be used to manage the response for all incidents and planned events.

ICS works! It saves lives!

Lesson Summary

Lesson 2: ICS Features and Principles

Lesson Overview

This lesson reviews ICS features and principles. At the end of this lesson, you should be able to:

- Describe the basic features of ICS.
- Select the correct terminology for ICS facilities.
- Identify common tasks related to personal accountability.

Making ICS Work

Effective incident management relies on a tight command and control structure for managing resources, making decisions, and assigning tasks. Although information is exchanged freely through the ICS structure, strict adherence must be paid to this top-down management approach when managing incidents in the field.

To make ICS work, each of us must commit to following this command and control approach.

ICS Features and Principles: Overview

As you learned in the previous lesson, ICS is based on proven management principles, which contribute to the strength and efficiency of the overall system.

ICS incorporates a wide range of management features and principles, beginning with the use of common terminology and clear text.

[David Burns, Emergency Preparedness Manager, University of California Los Angeles]
Communication is probably one of the most essential elements of ICS. It's important that we know how to communicate.

[Daryl Lee Spiewak, Emergency Programs Manager, the Brazos River Authority]
If the terms that I use mean different things to different people, we're going to have a hard time communicating and doing what needs to be done to accomplish our mission.

ICS emphasizes effective planning, including management by objectives and reliance on an Incident Action Plan.

[Roberta Runge, EPA National NIMS Coordinator]
You have to coordinate on what your end objective is. All up and down the chain you have to have a common end goal. So you can establish your objectives, you can ensure they're in the Incident Action Plan, and you can ensure that they are in agreement with the other Incident Action Plans that are produced by agencies.

The ICS features related to command structure include chain of command and unity of command.

[Bill Campbell, Director of Training, New York State Emergency Management Office]
One of the benefits is it gets all of the different organizations working under the same framework.

ICS helps ensure full utilization of all incident resources by:

- Maintaining a manageable span of control,
- Establishing predesignated incident locations and facilities,
- Implementing resource management practices, and
- Ensuring integrated communications.

ICS supports responders and decisionmakers through effective information and intelligence management and helps establish a common operating picture.

[Kristy Plourde, NIMS Program Coordinator, U.S. Coast Guard]
The common operating picture is a critical thing that the Coast Guard has been working hard on recently for ourselves because it's something that helps us maintain a better operational picture and it's more consistent across the board, everyone up and down the chain of command and across to other agencies understand the same picture.

ICS counts on each of us taking personal accountability for our own actions. And finally, the mobilization process helps ensure that incident objectives can be achieved while responders remain safe.

[Kristy Plourde, NIMS Program Coordinator, U.S. Coast Guard]
To have NIMS work effectively, it's got to be top-down support.

The ICS features covered in this lesson form the basis for effective, team-based incident response at all levels.

ICS Features and Principles: Overview

The remainder of this lesson covers the following ICS features and principles:

- Standardization
  - Common terminology
- Command
  - Establishment and transfer of command
  - Chain of command and unity of command
- Planning/Organizational Structure
  - Management by objectives
  - Incident Action Plan (IAP)
  - Modular organization
  - Manageable span of control

- Facilities and Resources
  - Comprehensive resource management
  - Incident locations and facilities
- Communications/Information Management
  - Integrated communications
  - Information and intelligence management
- Professionalism
  - Accountability
  - Dispatch/Deployment

Common Terminology and Clear Text

The ability to communicate within the ICS is absolutely critical. During an incident:

- Communications should use common terms or clear text.
- Do not use radio codes, agency-specific codes, acronyms, or jargon.

The goal is to promote understanding among all parties involved in managing an incident.

Why Plain English?

The following meanings of a common acronym illustrate the importance of using clear text.

EMT = Emergency Medical Treatment
EMT = Emergency Medical Technician
EMT = Emergency Management Team
EMT = Eastern Mediterranean Time (GMT+0200)
EMT = Effective Methods Team
EMT = Effects Management Tool
EMT = El Monte, CA (airport code)

EMT = Electron Microscope Tomography
EMT = Email Money Transfer

Command Definition

The next ICS principle is clarity of command or who is in charge. The National Incident Management System defines **command** as the act of directing, ordering, or controlling by virtue of explicit statutory, regulatory, or delegated authority.

When you are using ICS to manage an incident, an Incident Commander is assigned. The Incident Commander has the authority to establish objectives, make assignments, and order resources. In doing so, the Incident Commander works closely with staff and technical experts to analyze the situation and consider alternative strategies.

The Incident Commander should have the level of training, experience, and expertise to serve in this capacity. Qualifications to serve as an Incident Commander are not based on rank, grade, or technical expertise.

Chain of Command

Chain of command is an orderly line of authority within the ranks of the incident management organization. Chain of command:

- Allows an Incident Commander to direct and control the actions of all personnel under his or her supervision.
- Avoids confusion by requiring that orders flow from supervisors.

Chain of command does NOT prevent personnel from directly communicating with each other to ask for or share information.

Unity of Command

Under unity of command, personnel:

- Report to only one ICS supervisor.
- Receive work assignments only from their ICS supervisors.

When you are assigned to an incident, you no longer report directly to your day-to-day supervisor.

Transfer of Command

The process of moving the responsibility for incident command from one Incident Commander to another is called transfer of command. Transfer of command may take place when:

- A more qualified Incident Commander arrives and assumes command.
- A jurisdiction or agency is legally required to take command.
- The incident changes in complexity.

The transfer of command process always includes a transfer of command briefing, which may be oral, written, or a combination of both.

Management by Objectives

Incident objectives are used to ensure that everyone within the ICS organization has a clear understanding of what needs to be accomplished.

Incident objectives are established based on the following priorities:

1. Life Safety
2. Incident Stabilization
3. Property Preservation

Reliance on an Incident Action Plan

Every incident must have an Incident Action Plan (IAP) that:

- Specifies the incident objectives.
- States the activities to be completed.
- Covers a specified timeframe, called an operational period.
- May be **oral or written**—except for hazardous materials incidents, which require a written IAP.

Incident Action Plans specify the incident activities, assign responsibilities, identify needed resources, and specify communication protocols.

ICS Organization

The ICS organization is unique but easy to understand. There is no correlation between the ICS organization and the administrative structure of any single agency or jurisdiction. This is deliberate, because confusion over different position titles and organizational structures has been a significant stumbling block to effective incident management in the past.

For example, someone who serves as a director every day may not hold that title when deployed under an ICS structure.

Modular OrganizationThe ICS organizational structure:

- Develops in a top-down, modular fashion that is based on the size and complexity of the incident.
- Is determined based on the incident objectives and resource requirements. Only those functions or positions necessary for a particular incident are filled.
- Expands and contracts in a flexible manner. When needed, separate functional elements may be established.
- Requires that each element have a person in charge.

Manageable Span of Control

Another basic ICS feature concerns the supervisory structure of the organization. Maintaining adequate span of control throughout the ICS organization is very important.

Span of control pertains to the number of individuals or resources that one supervisor can manage effectively during an incident.

Maintaining an effective span of control is important at incidents where safety and accountability are a top priority.

Span of Control

The type of incident, nature of the task, hazards and safety factors, and distances between personnel and resources all influence span of control considerations.

Effective span of control on incidents may vary from three to seven, and a ratio of one supervisor to five subordinates is recommended.

Accounting for Incident Resources

In ICS, "resources" refers to personnel, supplies, and equipment. During an incident, it is critical to know:

- What resources are needed and available.
- Where deployed resources are located.

Effective resource management ensures that response personnel are safe and incident objectives are achieved.

Resource Management

Resource management includes processes for:

- Identifying resource requirements.
- Ordering and acquiring resources.
- Mobilizing and dispatching resources.
- Tracking and reporting on resource status.
- Recovering and demobilizing resources.

It also includes processes for reimbursing for resources and maintaining a resource inventory.

Predesignated Incident Locations and Facilities

Incident activities may be accomplished from a variety of operational locations and support facilities.

The Incident Commander identifies and establishes needed facilities depending on incident needs. Standardized names are used to identify types of facilities.

The most common type of facility you may encounter is the Incident Command Post. The Incident Command Post, or ICP, is the location from which the Incident Commander oversees all incident operations. The Command Post may be an office or resident post. The goal is to get you away from your day-to-day work setting so you will not be distracted from your incident assignments.

Incident Facilities Virtual Tour

This presentation introduces the ICS facilities. In less complex incidents you most likely will not need many of the standard ICS facilities. However, in large incidents, such as a hurricane or earthquake, it is likely that all of these facilities will be necessary.

The Incident Command Post, or ICP, is the location from which the Incident Commander oversees all incident operations. There should only be one ICP for each incident, but it may change locations during the event. Every incident must have some form of an Incident Command Post. The ICP may be located outside, in a vehicle, trailer, or tent, or within a building. The ICP will be positioned outside of the present and potential hazard zone but close enough to the incident to maintain command.

Staging Areas are temporary locations at an incident where personnel and equipment wait to be assigned. Staging Areas should be located close enough to the incident for a timely response, but far enough away to be out of the immediate impact zone. In large complex incidents, there may be more than one Staging Area at an incident. Staging Areas can be collocated with other ICS facilities.

A Base is the location from which primary logistics and administrative functions are coordinated and administered.

A Camp is the location where resources may be kept to support incident operations if a Base is not accessible to all resources. Camps are equipped and staffed to provide food, water, sleeping areas, and sanitary services.

A Helibase is the location from which helicopter-centered air operations are conducted. Helibases are generally used on a more long-term basis and include such services as fueling and maintenance.

Helispots are more temporary locations at the incident, where helicopters can safely land and take off. Multiple Helispots may be used.

Let's review the different ICS facilities covered in this video.

- The **Incident Command Post** is the location from which the Incident Commander oversees all incident operations.
- **Staging Areas** are where personnel and equipment are gathered while waiting to be assigned.
- A **Base** is the location from which primary logistics and administrative functions are coordinated and administered.
- A **Helibase** is the location from which helicopter-centered air operations are conducted.
- **Helispots** are more temporary locations at the incident, where helicopters can safely land and take off.

Incident Facilities

As you learned in the video presentation, standard ICS facilities include the following:

- **Incident Command Post:** The Incident Command Post is the location from which the Incident Commander oversees all incident operations.

Incident Command Post

On a map, the ICP location appears as a blue and white square.

- **Staging Area:** A Staging Area is a temporary location where personnel and equipment are gathered while waiting to be assigned.

Staging Area

On a map, the Staging

Base

On a map, the Base
appears as a circle
with a B in it.

- **Incident Base:** The Incident Base is the location from which primary logistics and administrative functions are coordinated and administered.

Camp, Helibase, and Helispot

- **Camp:** A Camp provides sleeping, food, water, and sanitary services to incident personnel.
- **Helibase:** A Helibase is a location from which helicopter-centered air operations are conducted.
- **Helispot:** A Helispot is a more temporary location at the incident, where helicopters can safely land and take off.

Remember, not all facilities are used in every incident. Also, if needed, additional types of facilities can be added to accommodate incident needs.

Integrated Communications

A common communications plan is essential for ensuring that personnel can communicate with one another during an incident.

Prior to an incident, response partners should work together to ensure that communication equipment, procedures, and systems can operate together during a response. This is known as interoperability.

Integrating communications can be as simple as making sure you have current phone numbers of all key players.

Information and Intelligence Management

The analysis and sharing of information and intelligence is an important component of ICS. Incident management must establish a process for gathering, sharing, and managing incident-related information and intelligence.

Intelligence includes operational information that may come from a variety of different sources, such as:

- Risk assessments.
- Threats involving potential for violence.
- Surveillance of disease outbreak.
- Weather forecasts.
- Structural plans and vulnerabilities.

Accountability

Effective accountability during incident operations is essential. Individuals must abide by their agency policies and guidelines and any applicable local, tribal, State, or Federal rules and regulations.

The following principles must be adhered to:

- **Check-In.** All responders must report in to receive an assignment.
- **Incident Action Plan.** Response operations must be coordinated as outlined in the Incident Action Plan.
- **Unity of Command.** Each individual will be assigned to only one supervisor.
- **Span of Control.** Supervisors must be able to adequately supervise and control their subordinates, as well as communicate with and manage all resources under their supervision.
- **Resource Tracking.** Supervisors must record and report resource status changes as they occur.

Dispatch/Deployment

A systematic deployment process improves safety and reduces chaos.

After being dispatched, your **first task is to check in and receive an assignment**.

After check-in, you will locate your incident supervisor and obtain your initial briefing. The briefings you receive and give should include:

- Current assessment of the situation and incident objectives.
- Identification of your specific job responsibilities.
- Description of ICS organizational structure and identification of coworkers.
- Location of work area.
- Identification of break areas, as appropriate.
- Procedural instructions for obtaining needed resources.
- Operational periods/work shifts.
- Required safety procedures and personal protective equipment (PPE), as appropriate.

Remember, you should respond only when dispatched by an appropriate authority.

ICS Features: Review

This lesson covered 14 ICS features that lay the foundation for effective response partnerships. The first seven ICS features are listed below:

1. **Common Terminology**

ICS establishes common terminology that allows diverse incident management and support organizations to work together across a wide variety of incident management functions and hazard scenarios. This common terminology covers the following:

- **Organizational Functions:** Major functions and functional units with incident management responsibilities are named and defined. Terminology for the organizational elements is standard and consistent.
- **Resource Descriptions:** Major resources—including personnel, facilities, and major equipment and supply items—that support incident management activities are given common names and are "typed" with respect to their capabilities, to help avoid confusion and to enhance interoperability.
- **Incident Facilities:** Common terminology is used to designate the facilities in the vicinity of the incident area that will be used during the course of the incident.

Incident response communications (during exercises and actual incidents) should feature plain language commands so they will be able to function in a multijurisdictional environment. Field manuals and training should be revised to reflect the plain language standard.

2. **Establishment and Transfer of Command**

The command function must be clearly established from the beginning of incident operations. The agency with primary jurisdictional authority over the incident designates the individual at the scene responsible for establishing command. When command is transferred, the process must include a briefing that captures all essential information for continuing safe and effective operations.

3. **Chain of Command and Unity of Command**

- **Chain of Command:** Chain of command refers to the orderly line of authority within the ranks of the incident management organization.
- **Unity of Command:** Unity of command means that all individuals have a designated supervisor to whom they report at the scene of the incident.

These principles clarify reporting relationships and eliminate the confusion caused by multiple, conflicting directives. Incident managers at all levels must be able to direct the actions of all personnel under their supervision.

4. **Unified Command**

In incidents involving multiple jurisdictions, a single jurisdiction with multiagency involvement, or multiple jurisdictions with multiagency involvement, Unified Command allows agencies with different legal, geographic, and functional authorities and responsibilities to work together effectively without affecting individual agency authority, responsibility, or accountability.

5. **Management by Objectives**

Management by objectives is communicated throughout the entire ICS organization and includes:

- Establishing overarching incident objectives.
- Developing strategies based on overarching incident objectives.
- Developing and issuing assignments, plans, procedures, and protocols.
- Establishing specific, measurable tactics or tasks for various incident management functional activities, and directing efforts to accomplish them, in support of defined strategies.
- Documenting results to measure performance and facilitate corrective actions.

6. **Incident Action Planning**

Centralized, coordinated incident action planning should guide all response activities. An Incident Action Plan (IAP) provides a concise, coherent means of capturing and communicating the overall incident priorities, objectives, and strategies in the contexts of both operational and support activities. Every incident must have an action plan. However, not all incidents require written plans. The need for written plans and attachments is based on the requirements of the incident and the decision of the Incident Commander or Unified Command. Most initial response operations are not captured with a formal IAP. However, if an incident is likely to extend beyond one operational period, become more complex, or involve multiple jurisdictions and/or agencies, preparing a written IAP will become increasingly important to maintain effective, efficient, and safe operations.

7. **Modular Organization**

The ICS organizational structure develops in a modular fashion based on the size and complexity of the incident, as well as the specifics of the hazard environment created by the incident. When needed, separate functional elements can be established, each of which may be further subdivided to enhance internal organizational management and external coordination. Responsibility for the establishment and expansion of the ICS modular organization ultimately rests with Incident Command, which bases the ICS organization on the requirements of the situation. As incident complexity increases, the organization expands from the top down as functional responsibilities are delegated. Concurrently with structural expansion, the number of management and supervisory positions expands to address the requirements of the incident adequately.

8. **Manageable Span of Control**

Span of control is key to effective and efficient incident management. Supervisors must be able to adequately supervise and control their subordinates, as well as communicate with and manage all resources under their supervision. In ICS, the span of control of any individual with incident management supervisory responsibility should range from 3 to 7 subordinates, with 5 being optimal. During a large-scale law enforcement operation, 8 to 10 subordinates may be optimal. The type of incident, nature of the task, hazards and safety factors, and distances between personnel and resources all influence span-of-control considerations.

9. **Comprehensive Resource Management**

Maintaining an accurate and up-to-date picture of resource utilization is a critical component of incident management and emergency response. Resources to be identified in this way include personnel, teams, equipment, supplies, and facilities available or potentially available for assignment or allocation.

0. **Incident Facilities and Locations**

Various types of operational support facilities are established in the vicinity of an incident, depending on its size and complexity, to accomplish a variety of purposes. The Incident Command will direct the identification and location of facilities based on the requirements of the situation. Typical designated facilities include Incident Command Posts, Bases, Camps, Staging Areas, mass casualty triage areas, point-of-distribution sites, and others as required.

1. **Integrated Communications**

Incident communications are facilitated through the development and use of a common communications plan and interoperable communications processes and architectures. The ICS 205 form is available to assist in developing a common communications plan. This integrated approach links the operational and support units of the various agencies involved and is necessary to maintain communications connectivity and discipline and to enable common situational awareness and interaction. Preparedness planning should address the equipment, systems, and protocols necessary to achieve integrated voice and data communications.

2. **Information and Intelligence Management**

The incident management organization must establish a process for gathering, analyzing, assessing, sharing, and managing incident-related information and intelligence.

3. **Accountability**

Effective accountability of resources at all jurisdictional levels and within individual functional areas during incident operations is essential. Adherence to the following ICS principles and processes helps to ensure accountability:

- Resource Check-In/Check-Out Procedures
- Incident Action Planning
- Unity of Command
- Personal Responsibility
- Span of Control
- Resource Tracking

4. **Dispatch/Deployment**

   Resources should respond only when requested or when dispatched by an appropriate authority through established resource management systems. Resources not requested must refrain from spontaneous deployment to avoid overburdening the recipient and compounding accountability challenges.

Lesson Summary

You have completed the ICS Features and Principles lesson. This lesson introduced:

- ICS management principles.
- ICS core system features.

The next lesson will provide an overview of the ICS organization and introduce the Incident Commander and Command Staff.

Lesson Summary

Lesson 3: Incident Commander and Command Staff Functions

Lesson Overview

This lesson introduces you to the roles of the Incident Commander and Command Staff functions. By the end of this lesson, you should be able to:

- Identify the five major ICS management functions.
- Describe the role and function of the Incident Commander.
- Describe the selection and transfer of Incident Commanders.
- Identify the position titles associated with the Command Staff.
- Describe the role and function of the Command Staff.

Performance of Management Functions

Every incident requires that certain management functions be performed. The problem must be identified and assessed, a plan to deal with it developed and implemented, and the necessary resources procured and paid for.

Regardless of the size of the incident, these same management functions are still required.

Five Major Management Functions

There are five major management functions that are the foundation upon which an incident management organization develops.

- Command
- Operations
- Planning
- Logistics
- Finance & Administration

These functions apply to incidents of all sizes and types, including planned events and emergencies that occur without warning.

Management Function Descriptions

Below is a brief description of the major incident management functions:

Command	Sets the incident objectives, strategies, and priorities and has overall responsibility for the incident.
Operations	Conducts operations to reach the incident objectives. Establishes tactics and directs all operational resources.
Planning	Supports the incident action planning process by tracking resources, collecting/analyzing information, and maintaining documentation.

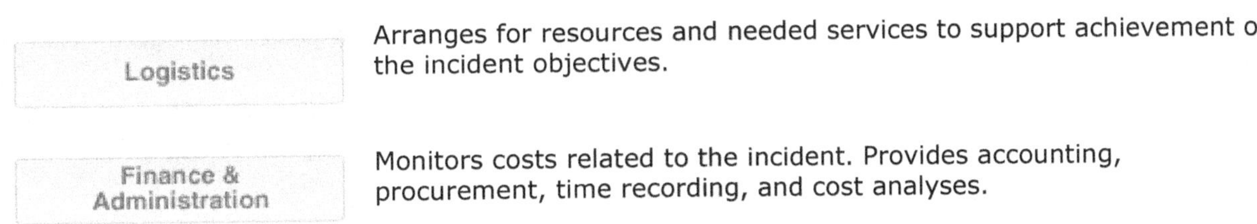

Incident Commander

The Incident Commander has overall responsibility for managing the incident by establishing objectives, planning strategies, and implementing tactics. The **Incident Commander is the only position that is always staffed in ICS applications.** On small incidents and events, one person—the Incident Commander—may accomplish all management functions.

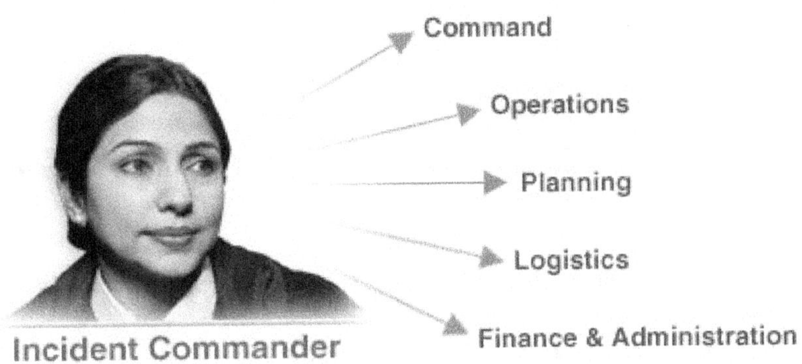

The Incident Commander is responsible for all ICS management functions until he or she delegates a function.

Delegating Incident Management Functions

As you learned in the previous lesson, the ICS organization is modular and has the capability to expand or contract to meet the needs of the incident. During a larger incident, the Incident Commander may create Sections and delegate the Operations, Planning, Logistics, and Finance/Administration functions.

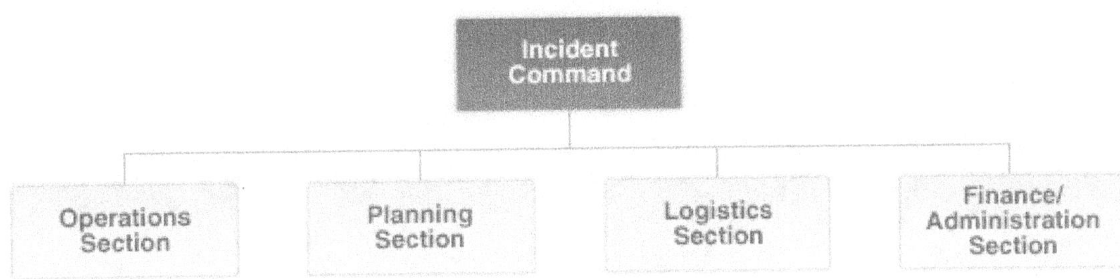

Remember . . . The Incident Commander only creates those Sections that are needed. If a Section is not staffed, the Incident Commander will personally manage those functions.

Incident Commander's Overall Role

The Incident Commander must have the authority to manage the incident and must be briefed fully. In some instances, a written delegation of authority should be established.

Personnel assigned by the Incident Commander have the authority of their assigned positions, regardless of the rank they normally hold within their organizations.

Incident Commander Responsibilities

In addition to having overall responsibility for managing the entire incident, the Incident Commander is specifically responsible for:

- Ensuring overall incident safety.
- Providing information services to internal and external stakeholders, such as disaster survivors, agency executives, and senior officials.
- Establishing and maintaining liaison with other agencies participating in the incident.

The Incident Commander may appoint one or more Deputies. **Deputy Incident Commanders must be as qualified as the Incident Commander.**

Selecting and Changing Incident Commanders

The Incident Commander is always a highly qualified individual trained to lead the incident response. Therefore, as an incident becomes more or less complex, command may change to meet the needs of the incident.

A formal transfer of command at an incident always requires a transfer of command briefing for the incoming Incident Commander.

Deputy Incident Commander

A Deputy Incident Commander may be designated to:

- Perform specific tasks as requested by the Incident Commander.
- Perform the incident command function in a relief capacity.
- Represent an assisting agency that shares jurisdiction.

Note that if a Deputy is assigned, he or she must be fully qualified to assume the Incident Commander's position.

Expanding the Organization

As incidents grow, the Incident Commander may delegate authority for performance of certain activities to the Command Staff and the General Staff. The Incident Commander will add positions only as needed.

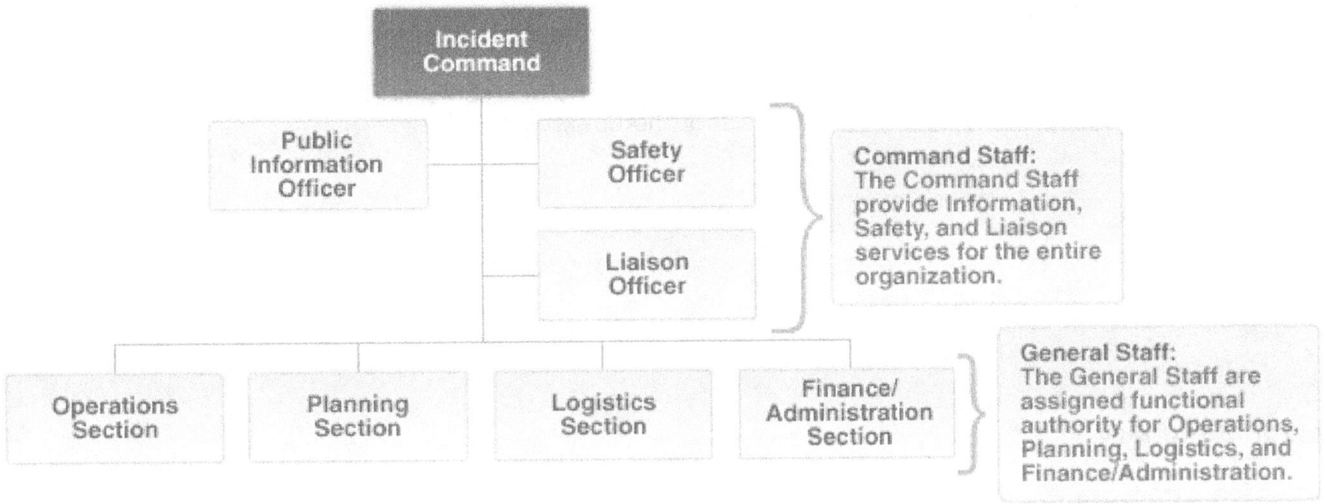

Command Staff Overview

You've now learned that the Incident Commander has overall authority and responsibility for conducting incident operations. An Incident Commander may assign staff to assist with managing the incident.

The Command Staff consists of the Public Information Officer, Safety Officer, and Liaison Officer, who all report directly to the Incident Commander.

Let's look at the roles of each member of the Command Staff. The Public Information Officer serves as the conduit for information to internal and external stakeholders, including the media and the public.

Accurate information is essential. The Public Information Officer serves as the primary contact for anyone who wants information about the incident and the response to it.

Another member of the Command Staff is the Safety Officer, who monitors conditions and develops measures for assuring the safety of all personnel.

The Safety Officer is responsible for advising the Incident Commander on issues regarding incident safety, conducting risk analyses, and implementing safety measures.

The final member of the Command Staff is the Liaison Officer, who serves as the primary contact for supporting agencies assisting at an incident.

Additionally, the Liaison Officer responds to requests from incident personnel for contacts among the assisting and cooperating agencies, and monitors incident operations in order to identify any current or potential problems between response agencies.

A Command Staff may not be necessary at every incident, but every incident requires that certain management functions be performed. An effective Command Staff frees the Incident Commander to assume a leadership role.

Review: Command Staff

Depending upon the size and type of incident or event, the Incident Commander may designate personnel to provide information, safety, and liaison services. In ICS, the following personnel comprise the Command Staff:

- **Public Information Officer**, who serves as the conduit for information to internal and external stakeholders, including the media, stakeholders, and the public.
- **Safety Officer**, who monitors safety conditions and develops measures for ensuring the safety of all incident personnel.

- **Liaison Officer**, who serves as the primary contact for other agencies assisting at an incident.

The Command Staff reports directly to the Incident Commander. In a complex incident, Assistant Officers may be assigned to each of the Command Staff functions.

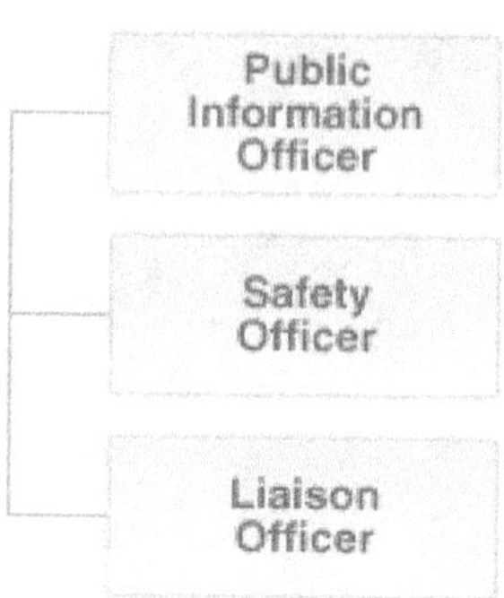

Lesson Summary

This lesson introduced you to the:

- Five major management functions.
- ICS organizational structure.
- Incident Commander roles and responsibilities.
- Selection and transfer of Incident Commanders.
- Command Staff roles and responsibilities.

The next lesson provides an introduction to the ICS General Staff.

Lesson Summary

Lesson 4: General Staff Functions

Lesson Overview

In the previous lesson, you learned that the Command Staff is responsible for overall management of the incident. This lesson introduces you to the General Staff. By the end of this lesson, you should be able to:

- Identify the ICS titles used for General Staff members.
- Describe the roles and functions of the four Sections.

General Staff

To maintain span of control, the Incident Commander may establish the following four Sections: Operations, Planning, Logistics, and Finance/Administration.

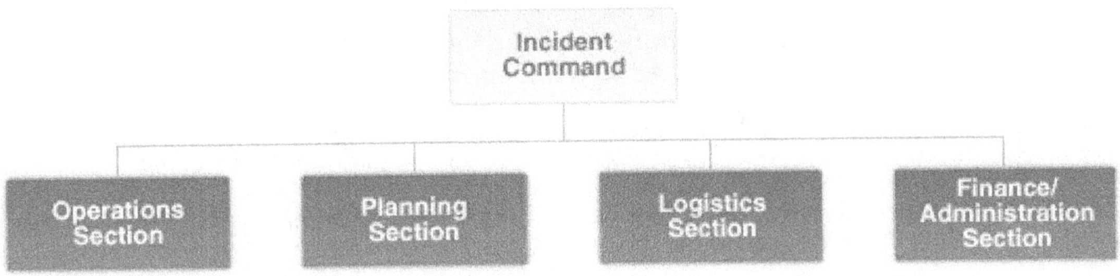

The General Staff, or Section Chiefs, report directly to the Incident Commander.

General Staff Overview

The General Staff overall responsibilities at an incident scene are summarized below:

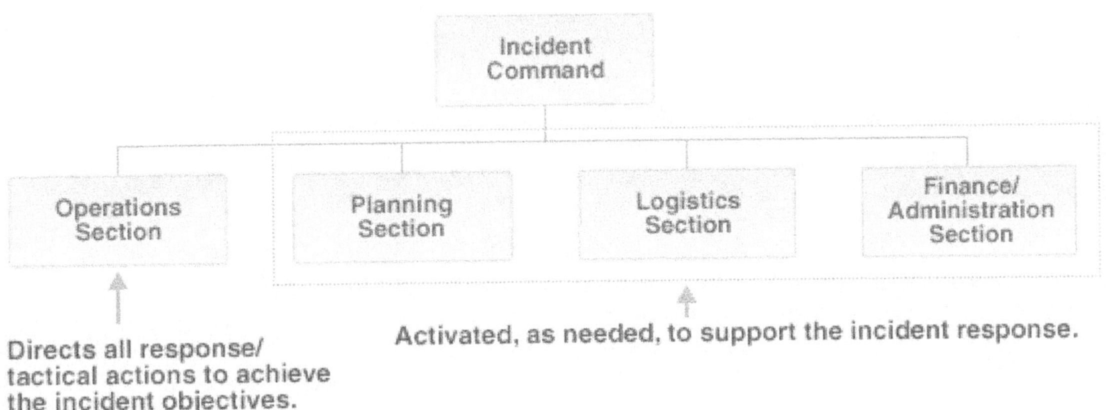

In an expanding incident, the Incident Commander first establishes the Operations Section. The remaining Sections are established as needed to support the operation.

ICS Position Titles: Review

ICS supervisory titles are important because they allow many different agencies to work together under a common organizational structure. Using consistent titles ensures that personnel from different organizations have the same credentials and qualifications. Let's review the ICS supervisory titles:

Organizational Level	Title	Support Position
Incident Command	Incident Commander	Deputy
Command Staff	Officer	Assistant
General Staff (Section)	Chief	Deputy
Branch	Director	Deputy
Division/Group	Supervisor	N/A
Unit	Leader	Manager
Strike Team/Task Force	Leader	Single Resource Boss

ICS Organizational Components

Section: The organizational level with responsibility for a major functional area of incident management (e.g., Operations, Planning, Logistics, Finance/Administration). The person in charge of each Section is designated as a Chief.

Division: The organizational level having responsibility for operations within a defined geographic area. The person in charge of each Division is designated as a Supervisor.

Group: An organizational subdivision established to divide the incident management structure into functional areas of operation. The person in charge of each Group is designated as a Supervisor.

Branch: An organizational level used when the number of Divisions or Groups exceeds the span of control. Can be either geographical or functional. The person in charge of each Branch is designated as a Director.

Task Force: A combination of mixed resources with common communications operating under the direct supervision of a Task Force Leader.

Strike Team: A set number of resources of the same kind and type with common communications operating under the direct supervision of a Strike Team Leader.

Single Resource: An individual, a piece of equipment and its personnel complement, or a crew or team of individuals with an identified supervisor that can be used at an incident.

Section Chiefs and Deputies

As mentioned previously, the person in charge of each Section is designated as a Chief. Section Chiefs have the ability to expand their Sections to meet the needs of the situation.

Each of the Section Chiefs may have a Deputy, or more than one, if necessary. The Deputy:

- May assume responsibility for a specific portion of the primary position, work as relief, or be assigned other tasks.
- Should always be as proficient as the person for whom he or she works.

When an incident involves multiple agencies, assigning Deputies from other organizations can increase interagency coordination.

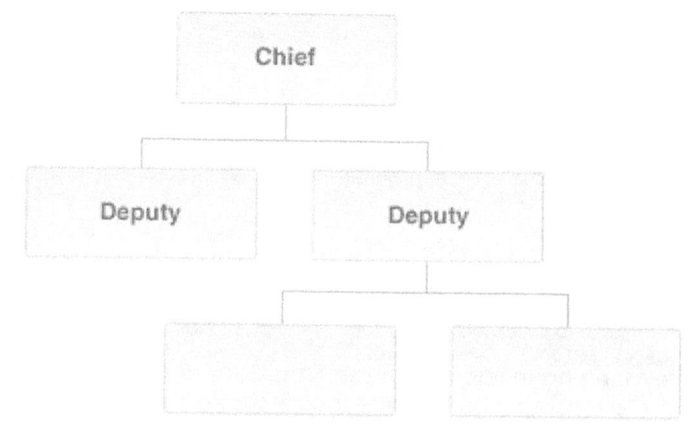

General Staff

As you previously learned, an Incident Commander is responsible for all incident management functions including: operations, planning, logistics, and finance and administration.

Depending on the incident needs, the Incident Commander may delegate some or all of these functions by establishing Sections. If a Section Chief is assigned to an incident, he or she will report directly to the Incident Commander.

Together, these Section Chiefs are referred to as the General Staff. Let's take a look at the responsibilities of each Section Chief.

The Operations Section Chief is responsible for developing and implementing strategy and tactics to accomplish the incident objectives. This means that the Operations Section Chief organizes, assigns, and supervises all the tactical or response resources assigned to the incident. Additionally, if a Staging Area is established, the Operations Section Chief would manage it.

The Planning Section Chief oversees the collection, evaluation, and dissemination of operational information related to the incident. It is the Planning Section's responsibility to prepare and disseminate the Incident Action Plan, as well as track the status of all incident resources.

The Planning Section helps ensure responders have accurate information and provides resources such as maps and floor plans.

The Logistics Section is responsible for providing facilities, services, and material support for the incident.

Logistics is critical on more complex incidents. The Logistics Section Chief assists the Incident Commander and Operations Section Chief by providing the resources and services required to support incident activities. During an incident, Logistics is responsible for ensuring the well-being of responders by providing sufficient food, water, and medical services. Logistics is also responsible for arranging communication equipment, computers, transportation, and anything else needed to support the incident.

Another critical function during complex incidents is Finance and Administration.

The Finance and Administration Section Chief is responsible for all of the financial and cost analysis aspects of an incident. These include contract negotiation, recording personnel and equipment time, documenting and processing claims for accidents and injuries occurring at the incident, and keeping a running tally of the costs associated with the incident.

We've now introduced you to the four ICS Sections.

It is important to remember that the ICS organizational structure is determined based on the incident objectives and resource requirements. It expands and contracts in a flexible manner. And, only those functions, positions, or sections necessary for a particular incident are filled.

Operations Section Chief

Typically, the Operations Section Chief is the person with the greatest tactical expertise in dealing with the problem at hand. The Operations Section Chief:

- Develops and implements strategy and tactics to carry out the incident objectives.
- Organizes, assigns, and supervises the tactical response resources.

Operations Section: Single Resources

Let's look at how resources are organized within the Operations Section. It all begins with Single Resources. Single Resources are individuals, a piece of equipment and its personnel complement, or a crew or team of individuals with an identified supervisor. On a smaller incident, the Operations Section may be comprised of an Operations Section Chief and single resources.

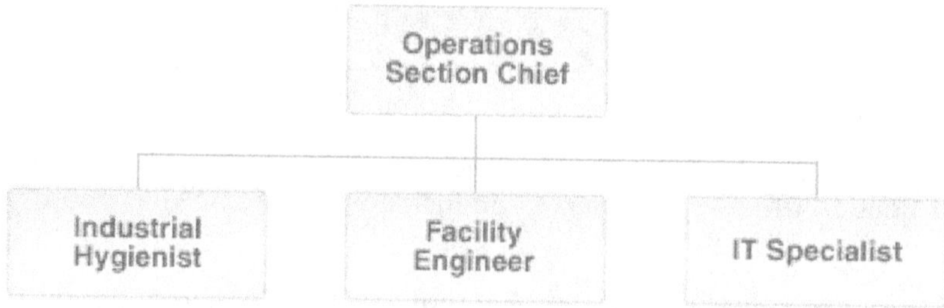

Operations Section: Teams

Single resources may be organized into teams. Using standard ICS terminology, the two types of team configurations are:

- **Task Forces** — A combination of **mixed resources** with common communications operating under the direct supervision of a Leader.
- **Strike Teams** — Consist of all **similar resources** with common communications operating under the direct supervision of a Leader.

Sample Strike Teams and Task Forces

The Operations Section organization chart shows possible team assignments in a flooding incident. Each team would have a Team Leader reporting to the Operations Section Chief.

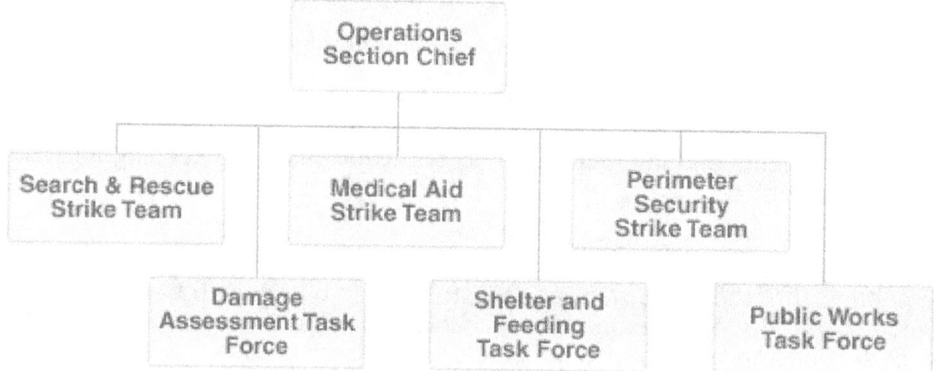

Note that these are examples of possible Strike Teams and Task Forces. These elements should be established based on the type of incident and unique requirements of the jurisdiction or agency.

Too Many Teams!

To maintain span of control, each team should be comprised of a Team Leader and no more than five to seven team members. As teams are added, what happens to the Operations Section Chief's span of control?

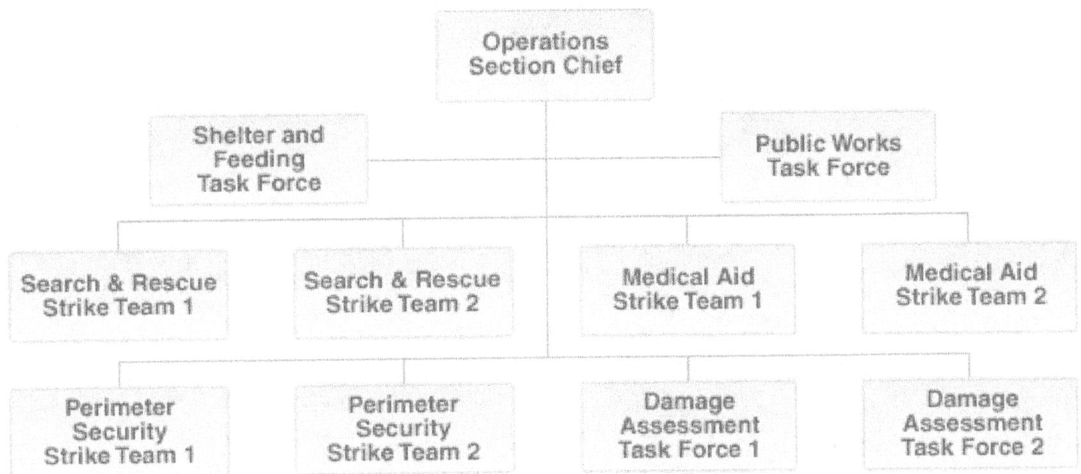

The Solution: Add Groups or Divisions

On a large, complex incident the Operations Section may become very large. Using the ICS principle of modular organization, the Operations Section may add the following elements to manage span of control:

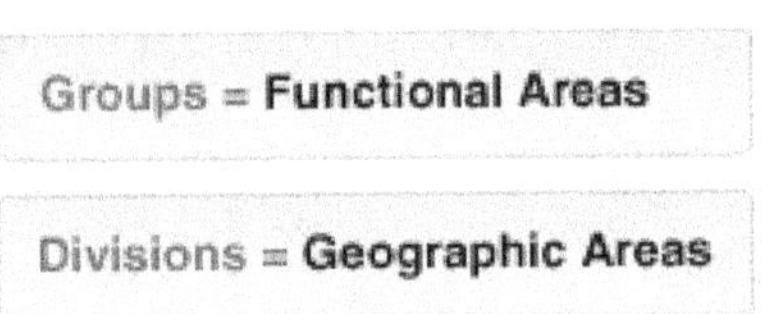

- **Groups** — Used to describe functional areas of operation.
- **Divisions** — Used to divide an incident geographically.

Maintaining Span of Control: Groups

The organization chart below illustrates how Groups can be used to maintain span of control within the Operations Section.

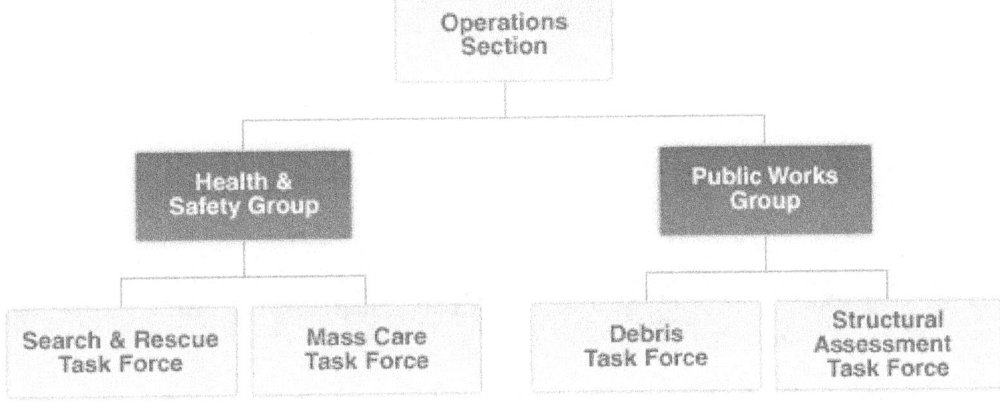

Maintaining Span of Control: Groups and Divisions (Geographic Areas)

The organization chart below illustrates how Groups and Divisions can be used together to maintain span of control within the Operations Section. The use of Divisions would be effective if the incident covered a large or isolated area of the community.

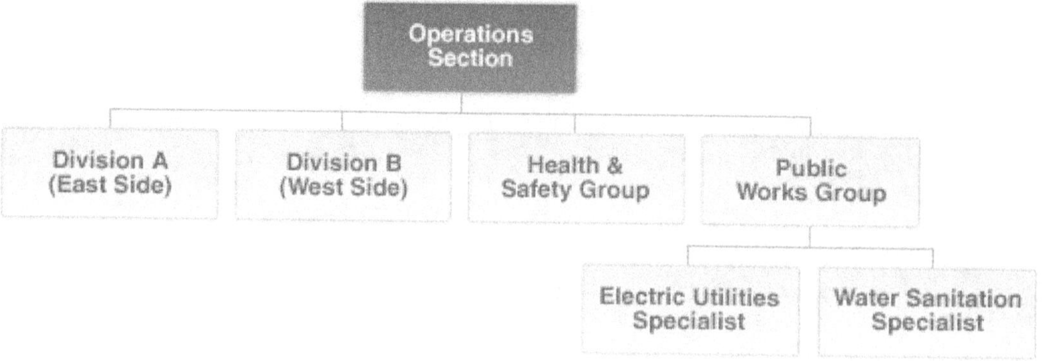

Operations Section: Establishing Branches

The Operations Section Chief may add Branches to supervise Groups and Divisions and further reduce his or her span of control.

The person in charge of each Branch is designated as a **Director**.

Review the chart. What are the advantages of reducing the Operations Section Chief's span of control?

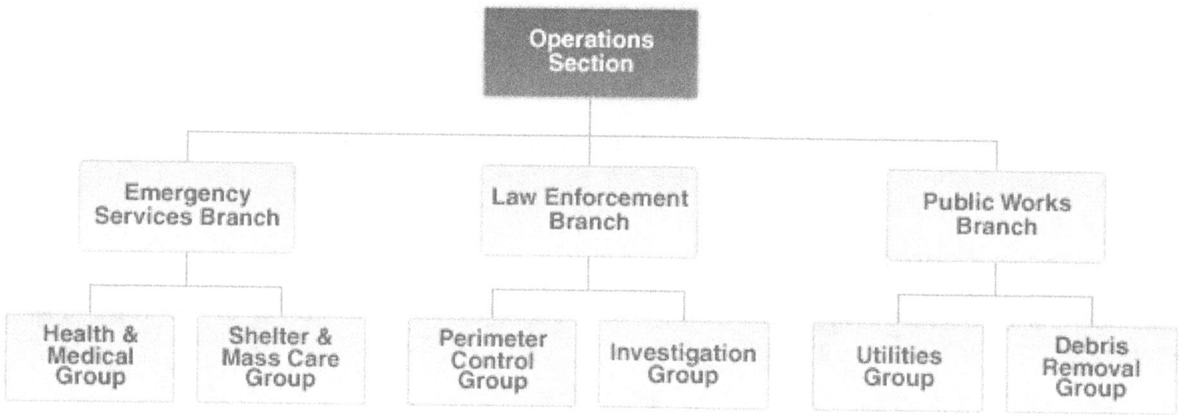

Planning Section

The Incident Commander will determine if there is a need for a Planning Section and, if so, will designate a Planning Section Chief.

If no Planning Section is established, the Incident Commander will perform all planning functions. It is up to the Planning Section Chief to activate any needed additional staffing.

Planning Section: Major Activities

The major activities of the Planning Section may include:

- Collecting, evaluating, and displaying incident intelligence and information.
- Preparing and documenting Incident Action Plans.
- Tracking resources assigned to the incident.
- Maintaining incident documentation.
- Developing plans for demobilization.

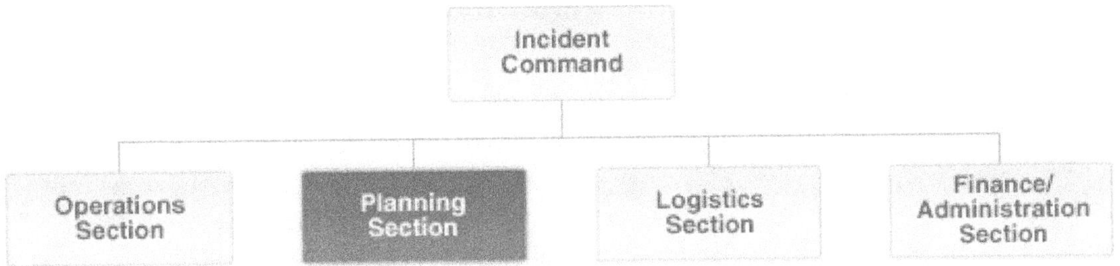

Planning Section Units

The Planning Section may include the following units:

Resources Unit: Responsible for recording the status of resources committed to the incident. This Unit also evaluates resources committed currently to the incident, the effects additional responding resources will have on the incident, and anticipated resource needs.

Situation Unit: Responsible for the collection, organization, and analysis of incident status information, and for analysis of the situation as it progresses.

Demobilization Unit: Responsible for ensuring orderly, safe, and efficient demobilization of incident resources.

Documentation Unit: Responsible for collecting, recording, and safeguarding all documents relevant to the incident.

Logistics Section

The Incident Commander will determine if there is a need for a Logistics Section at the incident, and if so, will designate an individual to fill the position of the Logistics Section Chief.

The Logistic Section Chief helps make sure that there are adequate resources (personnel, supplies, and equipment) for meeting the incident objectives. The Logistics Section Chief maintains his or her span of control by adding Branch Directors and Unit Leaders.

Logistics Section: Major Activities

The Logistics Section is responsible for all services and support needs, including:

- Ordering, obtaining, maintaining, and accounting for essential personnel, equipment, and supplies.
- Providing communication planning and resources.
- Setting up food services for responders.
- Setting up and maintaining incident facilities.
- Providing support transportation.
- Providing medical services to **incident personnel**.

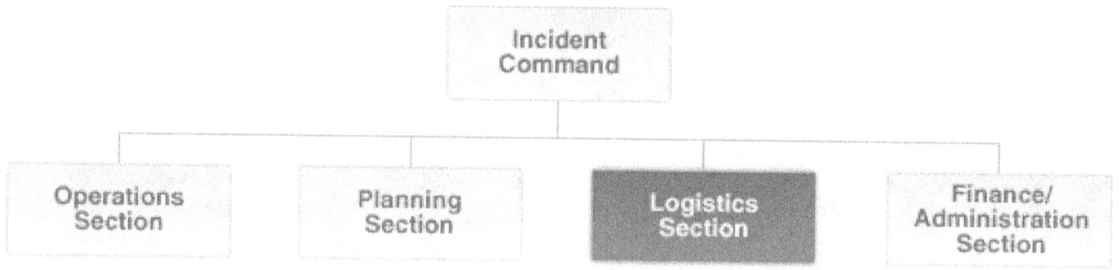

Logistics Section Units

Within the Logistics Section, the following six primary Units may be established:

Supply Unit: Orders, receives, stores, and processes all incident-related resources, personnel, and supplies.

Ground Support Unit: Provides all ground transportation during an incident. In conjunction with providing transportation, the Unit is also responsible for maintaining and supplying vehicles, keeping usage records, and developing incident Traffic Plans.

Facilities Unit: Sets up, maintains, and demobilizes all facilities used in support of incident operations. The Unit also provides facility maintenance and security services required to support incident operations.

Food Unit: Determines food and water requirements, plans menus, orders food, provides cooking facilities, cooks, serves, maintains food service areas, and manages food security and safety concerns.

Communications Unit: Major responsibilities include effective communications planning as well as acquiring, setting up, maintaining, and accounting for communications equipment.

Medical Unit: Responsible for the effective and efficient provision of medical services to incident personnel.

Finance/Administration Section

The Incident Commander will determine if there is a need for a Finance/Administration Section at the incident, and if so, will designate an individual to fill the position of the Finance/Administration Section Chief.

The Time, Compensation/Claims, Cost, and Procurement Units may be established within this Section.

Finance/Administration Section: Major Activities

The Finance/Administration Section is set up for any incident that requires incident-specific financial management. The Finance/Administration Section is responsible for:

- Contract negotiation and monitoring.
- Timekeeping.
- Cost analysis.
- Compensation for injury or damage to property.
- Documentation for reimbursement (e.g., under mutual aid agreements and assistance agreements).

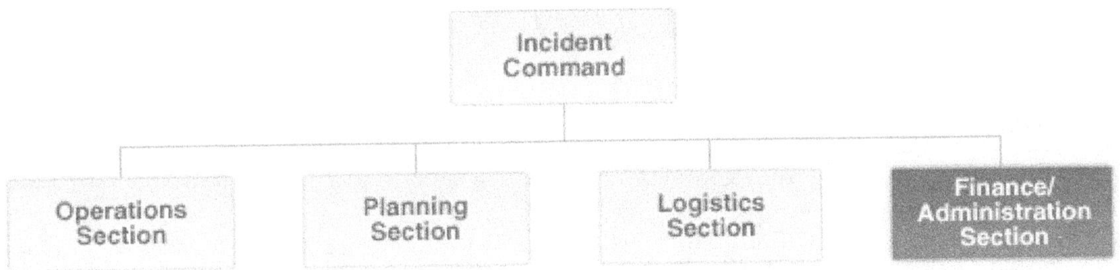

Finance/Administration Section Units

Within the Finance/Administration Section, the following four Units may be established:

Compensation/Claims Unit: Responsible for financial concerns resulting from property damage, injuries, or fatalities at the incident.

Cost Unit: Responsible for tracking costs, analyzing cost data, making estimates, and recommending cost savings measures.

Procurement Unit: Responsible for financial matters concerning vendor contracts.

Time Unit: Responsible for recording time for incident personnel and hired equipment.

Lesson Summary

This lesson introduced you to the General Staff, including:

- Roles and responsibilities.
- Position titles.

The next lesson focuses on how incidents are managed using Unified Command principles.

Lesson 5: Unified Command

Lesson Overview

The previous lessons covered Incident Command System (ICS) fundamentals. This lesson introduces you to the concepts of Unified Command and coordination.

By the end of this lesson, you should be able to:

- Define Unified Command.
- List the advantages of Unified Command.
- Differentiate between command and coordination.

Unified Command

The Unified Command organization consists of the Incident Commanders from the various jurisdictions or agencies operating together to form a single command structure in the field.

Unified Command Benefits

In a Unified Command, institutions and responding agencies blend into an integrated, unified team. A unified approach results in:

- A shared understanding of priorities and restrictions.
- A single set of incident objectives.
- Collaborative strategies.
- Improved internal and external information flow.
- Less duplication of efforts.
- Better resource utilization.

Incident Commanders Work Together

When implemented properly, Unified Command enables agencies with different legal, geographic, and functional responsibilities to coordinate, plan, and interact effectively.

The Incident Commanders within the Unified Command make joint decisions and speak as one voice. Any differences are worked out within the Unified Command.

Unity of command is maintained within the Operations Section. Each responder reports to a single supervisor within his or her area of expertise. Within a Unified Command, a police officer would not tell the firefighters how to do their job nor would the police direct search and rescue tactics.

Unified Command and NIMS

NIMS encourages the use of Unified Command.

"As a team effort, Unified Command allows all agencies with jurisdictional authority or functional responsibility for the incident to jointly provide management direction through a common set of incident objectives and strategies and a single Incident Action Plan. **Each participating agency maintains its authority, responsibility, and accountability**."

Unified Command Features

Co-located (Shared) Facilities

In a Unified Command, incident facilities are co-located or shared.

Bringing the responsible officials, Command Staffs, and planning elements together in a single Incident Command Post can promote coordination.

Single Planning Process and Incident Action Plan

Unified Command uses a single planning process and produces one Incident Action Plan. The planning process for Unified Command is similar to the process used on single-jurisdiction incidents.

Integrated General Staff

Integrating multijurisdictional and/or multiagency personnel into various other functional areas may be beneficial. For example:

- In Operations and Planning, Deputy Section Chiefs can be designated from an adjacent jurisdiction.
- In Logistics, a Deputy Logistics Section Chief from another agency or jurisdiction can help to coordinate incident support.

Incident Commanders within the Unified Command must concur on the selection of the General Staff Section Chiefs. The Operations Section Chief must have full authority to implement the tactics within the Incident Action Plan.

Coordinated Process for Resource Ordering

The Incident Commanders within the Unified Command work together to establish resource ordering procedures that allow for:

- Deployment of scarce resources to meet high-priority objectives.
- Potential cost savings through agreements on cost sharing for essential services.

Possible Unified Command Organization

Below is a possible Unified Command organizational structure for a hazardous materials incident.

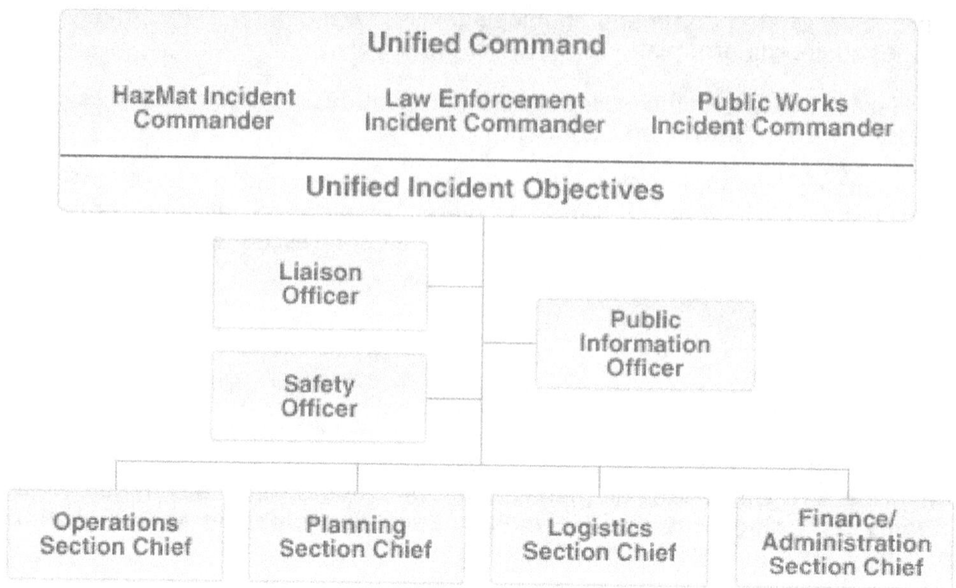

Incident Coordination

Coordination includes the activities that ensure that the onsite ICS organization receives the information, resources, and support needed to achieve the incident objectives. Coordination takes place in a number of entities and at all levels of government. Examples of coordination activities include:

- Establishing policy based on interactions with agency executives, other agencies, and stakeholders.
- Collecting, analyzing, and disseminating information to support the establishment of a common operating picture.
- Establishing priorities among incidents.
- Resolving critical resource issues.
- Facilitating logistics support and resource tracking.
- Synchronizing public information messages to ensure everyone is speaking with one voice.

Emergency Operations Center Role

Typically, an Emergency Operations Center (EOC) supports the on-scene response by relieving the Incident Commander of the burden of external coordination and securing additional resources.

An EOC is:

- A physical location.
- Staffed with personnel trained for and authorized to represent their agency/discipline.
- Equipped with mechanisms for communicating with the incident site and obtaining resources and potential resources.
- Managed through protocols.
- Applicable at different levels of government.

EOCs may be established at the Federal, State, tribal, and local levels.

Joint Information Center

Another coordination entity is the Joint Information Center (JIC). The JIC:

- May be established to coordinate all incident-related public information activities.
- Serves as the central point of contact for all news media. When possible, public information officials from all participating agencies should co-locate at the JIC.

JICs may be established at various levels of government or at incident sites.

Lesson Summary

This lesson familiarized you with Unified Command and coordination principles. Remember that:

- Unified Command enables agencies with different legal, geographic, and functional responsibilities to coordinate, plan, and interact effectively.
- Coordination provides strategic and policy guidance, information, and resource support, while the incident command structure in the field retains control of the incident operations and keeps policymakers and the EOC informed.

The next lesson provides tips on preparing to implement ICS principles.

IS-100.b - Intro to Incident Command System (ICS 100)

Lesson 1: Course Welcome & ICS Overview

Course Goal

The overall course goal is to promote effective response by:

- Familiarizing you with how Incident Command System (ICS) principles are used to manage incidents.
- Preparing you to coordinate with response partners from all levels of government and the private sector.

IS-100.b follows the National Incident Management System (NIMS) guidelines. To learn more about NIMS, you should complete IS-700.A, National Incident Management System, An Introduction.

Overall Course Objectives

At the completion of this course, you should be familiar with:

- ICS applications.
- ICS organizational principles and elements.
- ICS positions and responsibilities.
- ICS facilities and functions.
- ICS planning.

In addition, you will learn the steps you should take to be accountable for your actions during an incident.

What Is the Incident Command System?

The Incident Command System (ICS) is a standardized approach to incident management that:

- Enables a coordinated response among various jurisdictions and agencies.
- Establishes common processes for planning and managing resources.
- Allows for the integration of facilities, equipment, personnel, procedures, and communications operating within a common organizational structure.

Incident Command System: Helping Us Meet Our Mission

Disaster can strike anytime, anywhere. It takes many forms—a hurricane, an earthquake, a tornado, a flood, a fire or a hazardous spill, or an act of terrorism. An incident can build over days or weeks, or hit suddenly, without warning.

A poorly managed incident response can undermine our safety and well being. With so much at stake, we must effectively manage our response efforts.

Although most incidents are handled locally, partnerships among local, tribal, State, and Federal agencies as well as nongovernmental and private-sector organizations may be required.

As partners, we must respond together in a seamless, coordinated fashion.

The Incident Command System, or ICS, helps ensure integration of our response efforts. ICS is a standardized, on-scene, all-hazards approach to incident management. ICS allows all responders to adopt an integrated organizational structure that matches the complexities and demands of the incident while respecting agency and jurisdictional authorities. Although ICS promotes standardization, it is not without needed flexibility. For example, the ICS organizational structure can expand or contract to meet incident needs.

In this course, you'll learn ICS principles. And more importantly, you'll learn to interface better with your response partners.

Incident Command System Origins

The Incident Command System was developed in the 1970s following a series of catastrophic fires in California. Property damage ran into the millions, and many people died or were injured.

The personnel assigned to determine the causes of these disasters studied the case histories and discovered that response problems could rarely be attributed to lack of resources or failure of tactics.

Homeland Security Presidential Directives

- HSPD-5 identified steps for improved coordination in response to incidents. It requires the Department of Homeland Security (DHS) to coordinate with other Federal departments and agencies and State, local, and tribal governments to establish a National Response Framework (NRF) and a National Incident Management System (NIMS).
- PPD-8 - describes the Nation's approach to preparedness-one that involves the whole community, including individuals, businesses, community- and faith-based organizations, schools, tribes, and all levels of government (Federal, State, local, tribal and territorial).

NIMS and NRF

- NIMS provides a systematic, proactive approach to guide departments and agencies at all levels of government, nongovernmental organizations, and the private sector to work seamlessly to prevent, protect against, respond to, recover from, and mitigate the effects of incidents, regardless of cause, size, location, or complexity, in order to reduce the loss of life and property and harm to the environment.
- The NRF is a guide to how the Nation conducts all-hazards response – from the smallest incident to the largest catastrophe. This key document establishes a comprehensive, national, all-hazards approach to domestic incident response. The Framework identifies the key response principles, roles, and structures that organize national response. It describes how communities, States, the Federal Government, and private-sector and nongovernmental partners apply these principles for a coordinated, effective national response.

NIMS Components

NIMS is much more than just using the Incident Command System or an organization chart.

NIMS is a consistent, nationwide, systematic approach that includes the following components:

- **Preparedness**
  Actions taken to plan, organize, equip, train, and exercise to build and sustain the capabilities necessary to prevent, protect against, mitigate the effects of, respond to, and recover from those threats that pose the greatest risk. Within NIMS, preparedness focuses on the following elements: planning; procedures and protocols; training and exercises; personnel qualifications, licensure, and certification; and equipment certification.
- **Communications and Information Management**
  Emergency management and incident response activities rely on communications and information systems that provide a common operating picture to all command and coordination sites. NIMS describes the requirements necessary for a standardized framework for communications and emphasizes

the need for a common operating picture. This component is based on the concepts of interoperability, reliability, scalability, and portability, as well as the resiliency and redundancy of communications and information systems.

- **Resource Management**
  Resources (such as personnel, equipment, or supplies) are needed to support critical incident objectives. The flow of resources must be fluid and adaptable to the requirements of the incident. NIMS defines standardized mechanisms and establishes the resource management process to identify requirements, order and acquire, mobilize, track and report, recover and demobilize, reimburse, and inventory resources.

- **Command and Management**
  The Command and Management component of NIMS is designed to enable effective and efficient incident management and coordination by providing a flexible, standardized incident management structure. The structure is based on three key organizational constructs: the Incident Command System, Multiagency Coordination Systems, and Public Information.

- **Ongoing Management and Maintenance**
  Within the auspices of Ongoing Management and Maintenance, there are two components: the National Integration Center (NIC) and Supporting Technologies.

The components of NIMS were not designed to stand alone, but to work together.

Command and Management Elements

The NIMS Command and Management component facilitates incident management. This component includes the following elements: Incident Command System, Multiagency Coordination Systems, and Public Information.

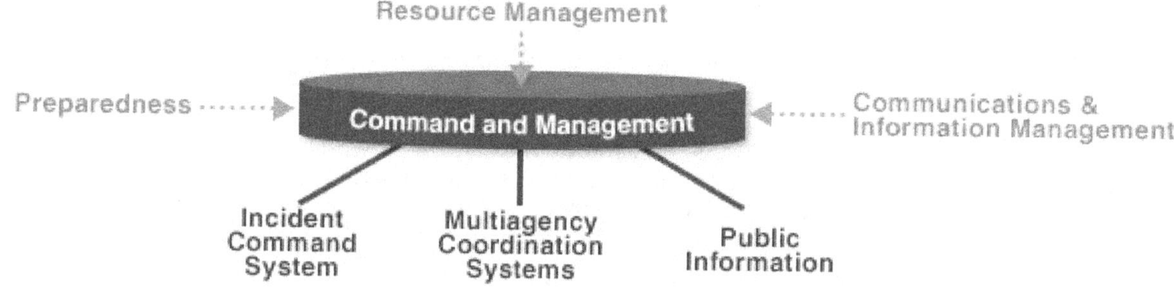

Lessons Learned

After-action reports from ineffective incident responses find that response problems are far more likely to result from inadequate management than from any other single cause. Weaknesses in incident management are often due to:

- Lack of accountability, including unclear chains of command and supervision.
- Poor communication, due to both inefficient uses of available communications systems and conflicting codes and terminology.
- Lack of an orderly, systematic planning process.
- No common, flexible, predesigned management structure that enabled commanders to delegate responsibilities and manage workloads efficiently.
- No predefined methods to integrate interagency requirements into the management structure and planning process effectively.

Using ICS enables us to avoid these weaknesses in all types of incident response.

Without ICS: Confusion and Poor Decisions

Without ICS, incident responses typically:

- Lack accountability, because of unclear chains of command and supervision.
- Have poor communications, due to both inefficient uses of available communications systems and conflicting codes and terminology.
- Use unsystematic planning processes and fail to reach objectives.
- Are unable to efficiently integrate responders into standard organizational structures and roles.

ICS: Built on Best Practices

ICS is based on decades of lessons learned. Using management best practices, ICS helps to ensure:

- The safety of responders, community members, and others.
- The achievement of response objectives.
- The efficient use of resources.

ICS has been tested in more than 30 years of emergency and nonemergency applications, by all levels of government and in nongovernmental and private–sector organizations.

When Is ICS Used?

ICS can be used to manage any type of incident, including a planned event (e.g., the Olympics, Presidential inauguration, etc.). The use of ICS is applicable to all hazards, including:

- **Natural Hazards:** Disasters, such as fires, tornadoes, floods, ice storms, earthquakes, foodborne illnesses, or epidemics.
- **Technological Hazards:** Dam breaks, radiological or hazmat releases, power failures, or medical device defects.
- **Human-Caused Hazards:** Criminal or terrorist acts , school violence, or other civil disturbances.

ICS: Not Just For Large-Scale Incidents

As a system, ICS is extremely useful. Not only does it provide an organizational structure for incident management, but it also guides the process for planning, building, and adapting that structure.

Using ICS for every incident or planned event helps improve and maintain skills needed for the large-scale incidents.

Lesson Summary

You have completed the ICS Overview lesson. This lesson presented the following key points:

- ICS is a standardized management tool that allows better coordination and use of resources.
- ICS represents organizational "best practices," and has become the standard for emergency management.
- ICS can be used to manage the response for all incidents and planned events.

ICS works! It saves lives!

Lesson 2: ICS Features and Principles

Lesson Overview

This lesson reviews ICS features and principles. At the end of this lesson, you should be able to:

- Describe the basic features of ICS.
- Select the correct terminology for ICS facilities.
- Identify common tasks related to personal accountability.

Making ICS Work

Effective incident management relies on a tight command and control structure for managing resources, making decisions, and assigning tasks. Although information is exchanged freely through the ICS structure, strict adherence must be paid to this top-down management approach when managing incidents in the field.

To make ICS work, each of us must commit to following this command and control approach.

ICS Features and Principles: Overview

As you learned in the previous lesson, ICS is based on proven management principles, which contribute to the strength and efficiency of the overall system.

ICS incorporates a wide range of management features and principles, beginning with the use of common terminology and clear text.

[David Burns, Emergency Preparedness Manager, University of California Los Angeles]
Communication is probably one of the most essential elements of ICS. It's important that we know how to communicate.

[Daryl Lee Spiewak, Emergency Programs Manager, the Brazos River Authority]
If the terms that I use mean different things to different people, we're going to have a hard time communicating and doing what needs to be done to accomplish our mission.

ICS emphasizes effective planning, including management by objectives and reliance on an Incident Action Plan.

[Roberta Runge, EPA National NIMS Coordinator]
You have to coordinate on what your end objective is. All up and down the chain you have to have a common end goal. So you can establish your objectives, you can ensure they're in the Incident Action Plan, and you can ensure that they are in agreement with the other Incident Action Plans that are produced by agencies.

The ICS features related to command structure include chain of command and unity of command.

[Bill Campbell, Director of Training, New York State Emergency Management Office]
One of the benefits is it gets all of the different organizations working under the same framework.

ICS helps ensure full utilization of all incident resources by:

- Maintaining a manageable span of control,
- Establishing predesignated incident locations and facilities,
- Implementing resource management practices, and
- Ensuring integrated communications.

ICS supports responders and decisionmakers through effective information and intelligence management and helps establish a common operating picture.

[Kristy Plourde, NIMS Program Coordinator, U.S. Coast Guard]
The common operating picture is a critical thing that the Coast Guard has been working hard on recently for ourselves because it's something that helps us maintain a better operational picture and it's more consistent across the board, everyone up and down the chain of command and across to other agencies understand the same picture.

ICS counts on each of us taking personal accountability for our own actions. And finally, the mobilization process helps ensure that incident objectives can be achieved while responders remain safe.

[Kristy Plourde, NIMS Program Coordinator, U.S. Coast Guard]
To have NIMS work effectively, it's got to be top-down support.

The ICS features covered in this lesson form the basis for effective, team-based incident response at all levels.

ICS Features and Principles: Overview

The remainder of this lesson covers the following ICS features and principles:

- Standardization
  - Common terminology
- Command
  - Establishment and transfer of command
  - Chain of command and unity of command
- Planning/Organizational Structure
  - Management by objectives
  - Incident Action Plan (IAP)
  - Modular organization
  - Manageable span of control
- Facilities and Resources
  - Comprehensive resource management
  - Incident locations and facilities
- Communications/Information Management
  - Integrated communications
  - Information and intelligence management
- Professionalism
  - Accountability
  - Dispatch/Deployment

Common Terminology and Clear Text

The ability to communicate within the ICS is absolutely critical. During an incident:

- Communications should use common terms or clear text.
- Do not use radio codes, agency-specific codes, acronyms, or jargon.

The goal is to promote understanding among all parties involved in managing an incident.

Why Plain English?

The following meanings of a common acronym illustrate the importance of using clear text.

EMT = Emergency Medical Treatment
EMT = Emergency Medical Technician
EMT = Emergency Management Team
EMT = Eastern Mediterranean Time (GMT+0200)
EMT = Effective Methods Team
EMT = Effects Management Tool
EMT = El Monte, CA (airport code)
EMT = Electron Microscope Tomography
EMT = Email Money Transfer

Command Definition

The next ICS principle is clarity of command or who is in charge. The National Incident Management System defines **command** as the act of directing, ordering, or controlling by virtue of explicit statutory, regulatory, or delegated authority.

When you are using ICS to manage an incident, an Incident Commander is assigned. The Incident Commander has the authority to establish objectives, make assignments, and order resources. In doing so, the Incident Commander works closely with staff and technical experts to analyze the situation and consider alternative strategies.

The Incident Commander should have the level of training, experience, and expertise to serve in this capacity. Qualifications to serve as an Incident Commander are not based on rank, grade, or technical expertise.

Chain of Command

Chain of command is an orderly line of authority within the ranks of the incident management organization. Chain of command:

- Allows an Incident Commander to direct and control the actions of all personnel under his or her supervision.
- Avoids confusion by requiring that orders flow from supervisors.

Chain of command does NOT prevent personnel from directly communicating with each other to ask for or share information.

Unity of Command

Under unity of command, personnel:

- Report to only one ICS supervisor.
- Receive work assignments only from their ICS supervisors.

When you are assigned to an incident, you no longer report directly to your day-to-day supervisor.

Transfer of Command

The process of moving the responsibility for incident command from one Incident Commander to another is called transfer of command. Transfer of command may take place when:

- A more qualified Incident Commander arrives and assumes command.
- A jurisdiction or agency is legally required to take command.
- The incident changes in complexity.

The transfer of command process always includes a transfer of command briefing, which may be oral, written, or a combination of both.

Management by Objectives

Incident objectives are used to ensure that everyone within the ICS organization has a clear understanding of what needs to be accomplished.

Incident objectives are established based on the following priorities:

1. Life Safety
2. Incident Stabilization
3. Property Preservation

Reliance on an Incident Action Plan

Every incident must have an Incident Action Plan (IAP) that:

- Specifies the incident objectives.
- States the activities to be completed.
- Covers a specified timeframe, called an operational period.
- May be **oral or written**—except for hazardous materials incidents, which require a written IAP.

Incident Action Plans specify the incident activities, assign responsibilities, identify needed resources, and specify communication protocols.

ICS Organization

The ICS organization is unique but easy to understand. There is no correlation between the ICS organization and the administrative structure of any single agency or jurisdiction. This is deliberate, because confusion over different position titles and organizational structures has been a significant stumbling block to effective incident management in the past.

For example, someone who serves as a director every day may not hold that title when deployed under an ICS structure.

Modular OrganizationThe ICS organizational structure:

- Develops in a top-down, modular fashion that is based on the size and complexity of the incident.
- Is determined based on the incident objectives and resource requirements. Only those functions or positions necessary for a particular incident are filled.
- Expands and contracts in a flexible manner. When needed, separate functional elements may be established.
- Requires that each element have a person in charge.

Manageable Span of Control

Another basic ICS feature concerns the supervisory structure of the organization. Maintaining adequate span of control throughout the ICS organization is very important.

Span of control pertains to the number of individuals or resources that one supervisor can manage effectively during an incident.

Maintaining an effective span of control is important at incidents where safety and accountability are a top priority.

Span of Control

The type of incident, nature of the task, hazards and safety factors, and distances between personnel and resources all influence span of control considerations.

Effective span of control on incidents may vary from three to seven, and a ratio of one supervisor to five subordinates is recommended.

Accounting for Incident Resources

In ICS, "resources" refers to personnel, supplies, and equipment. During an incident, it is critical to know:

- What resources are needed and available.
- Where deployed resources are located.

Effective resource management ensures that response personnel are safe and incident objectives are achieved.

Resource Management

Resource management includes processes for:

- Identifying resource requirements.
- Ordering and acquiring resources.
- Mobilizing and dispatching resources.
- Tracking and reporting on resource status.
- Recovering and demobilizing resources.

It also includes processes for reimbursing for resources and maintaining a resource inventory.

Predesignated Incident Locations and Facilities

Incident activities may be accomplished from a variety of operational locations and support facilities.

The Incident Commander identifies and establishes needed facilities depending on incident needs. Standardized names are used to identify types of facilities.

The most common type of facility you may encounter is the Incident Command Post. The Incident Command Post, or ICP, is the location from which the Incident Commander oversees all incident operations. The Command Post may be an office or resident post. The goal is to get you away from your day-to-day work setting so you will not be distracted from your incident assignments.

Incident Facilities Virtual Tour

This presentation introduces the ICS facilities. In less complex incidents you most likely will not need many of the standard ICS facilities. However, in large incidents, such as a hurricane or earthquake, it is likely that all of these facilities will be necessary.

The Incident Command Post, or ICP, is the location from which the Incident Commander oversees all incident operations. There should only be one ICP for each incident, but it may change locations during the event. Every incident must have some form of an Incident Command Post. The ICP may be located outside, in a vehicle, trailer, or tent, or within a building. The ICP will be positioned outside of the present and potential hazard zone but close enough to the incident to maintain command.

Staging Areas are temporary locations at an incident where personnel and equipment wait to be assigned. Staging Areas should be located close enough to the incident for a timely response, but far enough away to be out of the immediate impact zone. In large complex incidents, there may be more than one Staging Area at an incident. Staging Areas can be collocated with other ICS facilities.

A Base is the location from which primary logistics and administrative functions are coordinated and administered.

A Camp is the location where resources may be kept to support incident operations if a Base is not accessible to all resources. Camps are equipped and staffed to provide food, water, sleeping areas, and sanitary services.

A Helibase is the location from which helicopter-centered air operations are conducted. Helibases are generally used on a more long-term basis and include such services as fueling and maintenance.

Helispots are more temporary locations at the incident, where helicopters can safely land and take off. Multiple Helispots may be used.

Let's review the different ICS facilities covered in this video.

- The **Incident Command Post** is the location from which the Incident Commander oversees all incident operations.
- **Staging Areas** are where personnel and equipment are gathered while waiting to be assigned.
- A **Base** is the location from which primary logistics and administrative functions are coordinated and administered.
- A **Helibase** is the location from which helicopter-centered air operations are conducted.
- **Helispots** are more temporary locations at the incident, where helicopters can safely land and take off.

Incident Facilities

As you learned in the video presentation, standard ICS facilities include the following:

- **Incident Command Post:** The Incident Command Post is the location from which the Incident Commander oversees all incident operations.

Incident Command Post

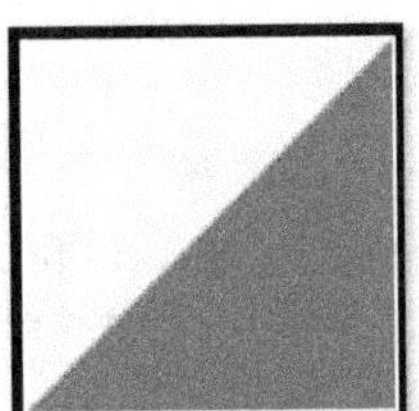

On a map, the ICP location appears as a blue and white square.

- **Staging Area:** A Staging Area is a temporary location where personnel and equipment are gathered while waiting to be assigned.

Staging Area

On a map, the Staging Area appears as a circle with an S in it.

- **Incident Base:** The Incident Base is the location from which primary logistics and administrative functions are coordinated and administered.

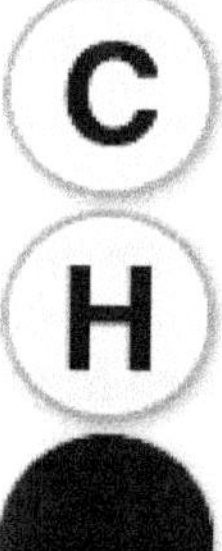

- **Camp:** A Camp provides sleeping, food, water, and sanitary services to incident personnel.
- **Helibase:** A Helibase is a location from which helicopter-centered air operations are conducted.
- **Helispot:** A Helispot is a more temporary location at the incident, where helicopters can safely land and take off.

Remember, not all facilities are used in every incident. Also, if needed, additional types of facilities can be added to accommodate incident needs.

Integrated Communications

A common communications plan is essential for ensuring that personnel can communicate with one another during an incident.

Prior to an incident, response partners should work together to ensure that communication equipment, procedures, and systems can operate together during a response. This is known as interoperability.

Integrating communications can be as simple as making sure you have current phone numbers of all key players.

Information and Intelligence Management

The analysis and sharing of information and intelligence is an important component of ICS. Incident management must establish a process for gathering, sharing, and managing incident-related information and intelligence.

Intelligence includes operational information that may come from a variety of different sources, such as:

- Risk assessments.

- Threats involving potential for violence.
- Surveillance of disease outbreak.
- Weather forecasts.
- Structural plans and vulnerabilities.

Accountability

Effective accountability during incident operations is essential. Individuals must abide by their agency policies and guidelines and any applicable local, tribal, State, or Federal rules and regulations.

The following principles must be adhered to:

- **Check-In.** All responders must report in to receive an assignment.
- **Incident Action Plan.** Response operations must be coordinated as outlined in the Incident Action Plan.
- **Unity of Command.** Each individual will be assigned to only one supervisor.
- **Span of Control.** Supervisors must be able to adequately supervise and control their subordinates, as well as communicate with and manage all resources under their supervision.
- **Resource Tracking.** Supervisors must record and report resource status changes as they occur.

Dispatch/Deployment

A systematic deployment process improves safety and reduces chaos.

After being dispatched, your **first task is to check in and receive an assignment**.

After check-in, you will locate your incident supervisor and obtain your initial briefing. The briefings you receive and give should include:

- Current assessment of the situation and incident objectives.
- Identification of your specific job responsibilities.
- Description of ICS organizational structure and identification of coworkers.
- Location of work area.
- Identification of break areas, as appropriate.
- Procedural instructions for obtaining needed resources.
- Operational periods/work shifts.
- Required safety procedures and personal protective equipment (PPE), as appropriate.

Remember, you should respond only when dispatched by an appropriate authority.

ICS Features: Review

This lesson covered 14 ICS features that lay the foundation for effective response partnerships. The first seven ICS features are listed below:

1. **Common Terminology**

   ICS establishes common terminology that allows diverse incident management and support organizations to work together across a wide variety of incident management functions and hazard scenarios. This common terminology covers the following:

   - **Organizational Functions:** Major functions and functional units with incident management responsibilities are named and defined. Terminology for the organizational elements is standard and consistent.

- **Resource Descriptions:** Major resources—including personnel, facilities, and major equipment and supply items—that support incident management activities are given common names and are "typed" with respect to their capabilities, to help avoid confusion and to enhance interoperability.
- **Incident Facilities:** Common terminology is used to designate the facilities in the vicinity of the incident area that will be used during the course of the incident.

Incident response communications (during exercises and actual incidents) should feature plain language commands so they will be able to function in a multijurisdictional environment. Field manuals and training should be revised to reflect the plain language standard.

2. **Establishment and Transfer of Command**

   The command function must be clearly established from the beginning of incident operations. The agency with primary jurisdictional authority over the incident designates the individual at the scene responsible for establishing command. When command is transferred, the process must include a briefing that captures all essential information for continuing safe and effective operations.

3. **Chain of Command and Unity of Command**

   - **Chain of Command:** Chain of command refers to the orderly line of authority within the ranks of the incident management organization.
   - **Unity of Command:** Unity of command means that all individuals have a designated supervisor to whom they report at the scene of the incident.

   These principles clarify reporting relationships and eliminate the confusion caused by multiple, conflicting directives. Incident managers at all levels must be able to direct the actions of all personnel under their supervision.

4. **Unified Command**

   In incidents involving multiple jurisdictions, a single jurisdiction with multiagency involvement, or multiple jurisdictions with multiagency involvement, Unified Command allows agencies with different legal, geographic, and functional authorities and responsibilities to work together effectively without affecting individual agency authority, responsibility, or accountability.

5. **Management by Objectives**

   Management by objectives is communicated throughout the entire ICS organization and includes:

   - Establishing overarching incident objectives.
   - Developing strategies based on overarching incident objectives.
   - Developing and issuing assignments, plans, procedures, and protocols.
   - Establishing specific, measurable tactics or tasks for various incident management functional activities, and directing efforts to accomplish them, in support of defined strategies.
   - Documenting results to measure performance and facilitate corrective actions.

6. **Incident Action Planning**

   Centralized, coordinated incident action planning should guide all response activities. An Incident Action Plan (IAP) provides a concise, coherent means of capturing and communicating the overall incident priorities, objectives, and strategies in the contexts of both operational and support activities. Every incident must have an action plan. However, not all incidents require written plans. The need for written plans and attachments is based on the requirements of the incident and the decision of the Incident Commander or Unified Command. Most initial response operations are not captured with a formal IAP. However, if an incident is likely to extend beyond one operational period, become more complex, or involve multiple jurisdictions and/or agencies, preparing a written IAP will become increasingly important to maintain effective, efficient, and safe operations.

7. **Modular Organization**

   The ICS organizational structure develops in a modular fashion based on the size and complexity of the incident, as well as the specifics of the hazard environment created by the incident. When needed, separate functional elements can be established, each of which may be further subdivided to enhance internal organizational management and external coordination. Responsibility for the establishment and expansion of the ICS modular organization ultimately rests with Incident Command, which bases the

ICS organization on the requirements of the situation. As incident complexity increases, the organization expands from the top down as functional responsibilities are delegated. Concurrently with structural expansion, the number of management and supervisory positions expands to address the requirements of the incident adequately.

8. **Manageable Span of Control**

Span of control is key to effective and efficient incident management. Supervisors must be able to adequately supervise and control their subordinates, as well as communicate with and manage all resources under their supervision. In ICS, the span of control of any individual with incident management supervisory responsibility should range from 3 to 7 subordinates, with 5 being optimal. During a large-scale law enforcement operation, 8 to 10 subordinates may be optimal. The type of incident, nature of the task, hazards and safety factors, and distances between personnel and resources all influence span-of-control considerations.

9. **Comprehensive Resource Management**

Maintaining an accurate and up-to-date picture of resource utilization is a critical component of incident management and emergency response. Resources to be identified in this way include personnel, teams, equipment, supplies, and facilities available or potentially available for assignment or allocation.

0. **Incident Facilities and Locations**

Various types of operational support facilities are established in the vicinity of an incident, depending on its size and complexity, to accomplish a variety of purposes. The Incident Command will direct the identification and location of facilities based on the requirements of the situation. Typical designated facilities include Incident Command Posts, Bases, Camps, Staging Areas, mass casualty triage areas, point-of-distribution sites, and others as required.

1. **Integrated Communications**

Incident communications are facilitated through the development and use of a common communications plan and interoperable communications processes and architectures. The ICS 205 form is available to assist in developing a common communications plan. This integrated approach links the operational and support units of the various agencies involved and is necessary to maintain communications connectivity and discipline and to enable common situational awareness and interaction. Preparedness planning should address the equipment, systems, and protocols necessary to achieve integrated voice and data communications.

2. **Information and Intelligence Management**

The incident management organization must establish a process for gathering, analyzing, assessing, sharing, and managing incident-related information and intelligence.

3. **Accountability**

Effective accountability of resources at all jurisdictional levels and within individual functional areas during incident operations is essential. Adherence to the following ICS principles and processes helps to ensure accountability:

- Resource Check-In/Check-Out Procedures
- Incident Action Planning
- Unity of Command
- Personal Responsibility
- Span of Control
- Resource Tracking

4. **Dispatch/Deployment**

Resources should respond only when requested or when dispatched by an appropriate authority through established resource management systems. Resources not requested must refrain from spontaneous deployment to avoid overburdening the recipient and compounding accountability challenges.

Lesson Summary

You have completed the ICS Features and Principles lesson. This lesson introduced:

- ICS management principles.
- ICS core system features.

The next lesson will provide an overview of the ICS organization and introduce the Incident Commander and Command Staff.

Lesson 3: Incident Commander and Command Staff Functions

Lesson Overview

This lesson introduces you to the roles of the Incident Commander and Command Staff functions. By the end of this lesson, you should be able to:

- Identify the five major ICS management functions.
- Describe the role and function of the Incident Commander.
- Describe the selection and transfer of Incident Commanders.
- Identify the position titles associated with the Command Staff.
- Describe the role and function of the Command Staff.

Performance of Management Functions

Every incident requires that certain management functions be performed. The problem must be identified and assessed, a plan to deal with it developed and implemented, and the necessary resources procured and paid for.

Regardless of the size of the incident, these same management functions are still required.

Five Major Management Functions

There are five major management functions that are the foundation upon which an incident management organization develops.

- Command
- Operations
- Planning
- Logistics
- Finance & Administration

These functions apply to incidents of all sizes and types, including planned events and emergencies that occur without warning.

Management Function Descriptions

Below is a brief description of the major incident management functions:

Sets the incident objectives, strategies, and priorities and has overall responsibility for the incident.

| Operations | Conducts operations to reach the incident objectives. Establishes tactics and directs all operational resources. |

| Planning | Supports the incident action planning process by tracking resources, collecting/analyzing information, and maintaining documentation. |

| Logistics | Arranges for resources and needed services to support achievement of the incident objectives. |

| Finance & Administration | Monitors costs related to the incident. Provides accounting, procurement, time recording, and cost analyses. |

Incident Commander

The Incident Commander has overall responsibility for managing the incident by establishing objectives, planning strategies, and implementing tactics. The **Incident Commander is the only position that is always staffed in ICS applications.** On small incidents and events, one person—the Incident Commander—may accomplish all management functions.

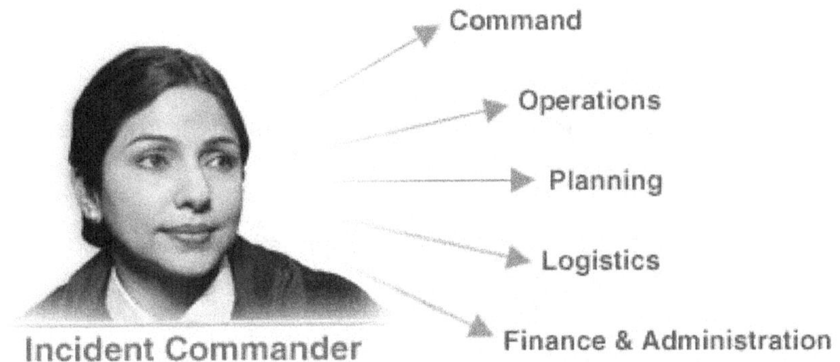

Incident Commander

The Incident Commander is responsible for all ICS management functions until he or she delegates a function.

Delegating Incident Management Functions

As you learned in the previous lesson, the ICS organization is modular and has the capability to expand or contract to meet the needs of the incident. During a larger incident, the Incident Commander may create Sections and delegate the Operations, Planning, Logistics, and Finance/Administration functions.

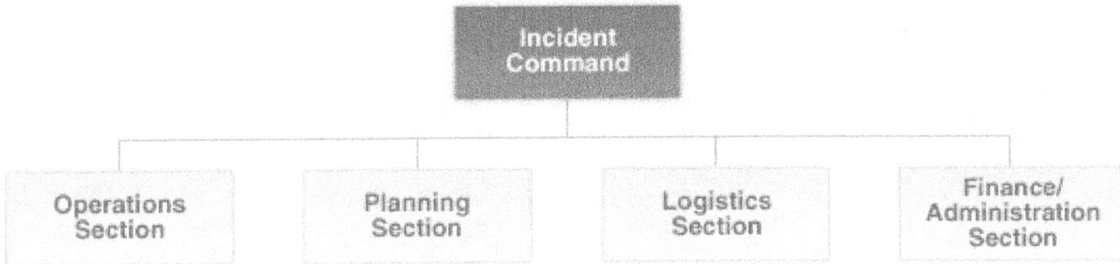

Remember . . . The Incident Commander only creates those Sections that are needed. If a Section is not staffed, the Incident Commander will personally manage those functions.

Incident Commander's Overall Role

The Incident Commander must have the authority to manage the incident and must be briefed fully. In some instances, a written delegation of authority should be established.

Personnel assigned by the Incident Commander have the authority of their assigned positions, regardless of the rank they normally hold within their organizations.

Incident Commander Responsibilities

In addition to having overall responsibility for managing the entire incident, the Incident Commander is specifically responsible for:

- Ensuring overall incident safety.
- Providing information services to internal and external stakeholders, such as disaster survivors, agency executives, and senior officials.
- Establishing and maintaining liaison with other agencies participating in the incident.

The Incident Commander may appoint one or more Deputies. **Deputy Incident Commanders must be as qualified as the Incident Commander.**

Selecting and Changing Incident Commanders

The Incident Commander is always a highly qualified individual trained to lead the incident response. Therefore, as an incident becomes more or less complex, command may change to meet the needs of the incident.

A formal transfer of command at an incident always requires a transfer of command briefing for the incoming Incident Commander.

Deputy Incident Commander

A Deputy Incident Commander may be designated to:

- Perform specific tasks as requested by the Incident Commander.
- Perform the incident command function in a relief capacity.
- Represent an assisting agency that shares jurisdiction.

Note that if a Deputy is assigned, he or she must be fully qualified to assume the Incident Commander's position.

Expanding the Organization

As incidents grow, the Incident Commander may delegate authority for performance of certain activities to the Command Staff and the General Staff. The Incident Commander will add positions only as needed.

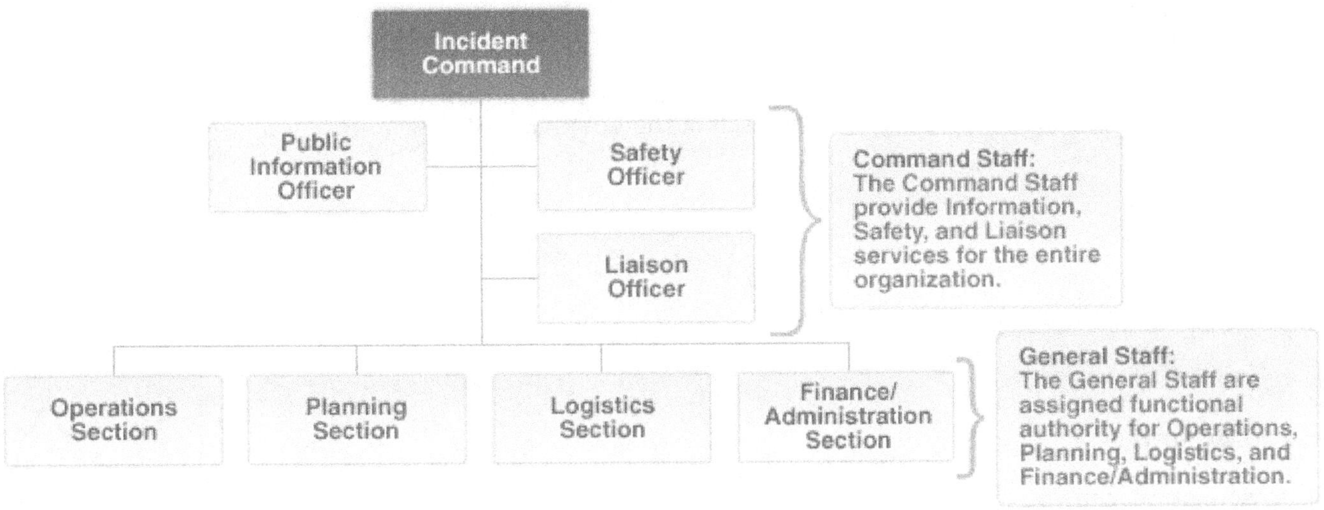

Command Staff Overview

You've now learned that the Incident Commander has overall authority and responsibility for conducting incident operations. An Incident Commander may assign staff to assist with managing the incident.

The Command Staff consists of the Public Information Officer, Safety Officer, and Liaison Officer, who all report directly to the Incident Commander.

Let's look at the roles of each member of the Command Staff. The Public Information Officer serves as the conduit for information to internal and external stakeholders, including the media and the public.

Accurate information is essential. The Public Information Officer serves as the primary contact for anyone who wants information about the incident and the response to it.

Another member of the Command Staff is the Safety Officer, who monitors conditions and develops measures for assuring the safety of all personnel.

The Safety Officer is responsible for advising the Incident Commander on issues regarding incident safety, conducting risk analyses, and implementing safety measures.

The final member of the Command Staff is the Liaison Officer, who serves as the primary contact for supporting agencies assisting at an incident.

Additionally, the Liaison Officer responds to requests from incident personnel for contacts among the assisting and cooperating agencies, and monitors incident operations in order to identify any current or potential problems between response agencies.

A Command Staff may not be necessary at every incident, but every incident requires that certain management functions be performed. An effective Command Staff frees the Incident Commander to assume a leadership role.

Review: Command Staff

Depending upon the size and type of incident or event, the Incident Commander may designate personnel to provide information, safety, and liaison services. In ICS, the following personnel comprise the Command Staff:

- **Public Information Officer**, who serves as the conduit for information to internal and external stakeholders, including the media, stakeholders, and the public.
- **Safety Officer**, who monitors safety conditions and develops measures for ensuring the safety of all incident personnel.

- **Liaison Officer**, who serves as the primary contact for other agencies assisting at an incident.

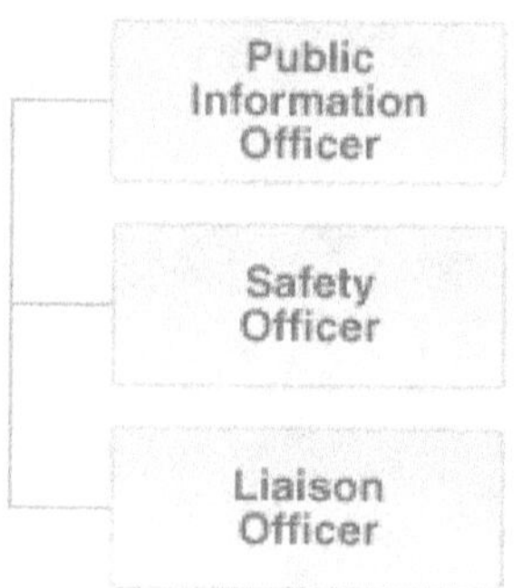

The Command Staff reports directly to the Incident Commander. In a complex incident, Assistant Officers may be assigned to each of the Command Staff functions.

Lesson Summary

This lesson introduced you to the:

- Five major management functions.
- ICS organizational structure.
- Incident Commander roles and responsibilities.
- Selection and transfer of Incident Commanders.
- Command Staff roles and responsibilities.

The next lesson provides an introduction to the ICS General Staff.

Lesson 4: General Staff Functions

Lesson Overview

In the previous lesson, you learned that the Command Staff is responsible for overall management of the incident. This lesson introduces you to the General Staff. By the end of this lesson, you should be able to:

- Identify the ICS titles used for General Staff members.
- Describe the roles and functions of the four Sections.

General Staff

To maintain span of control, the Incident Commander may establish the following four Sections: Operations, Planning, Logistics, and Finance/Administration.

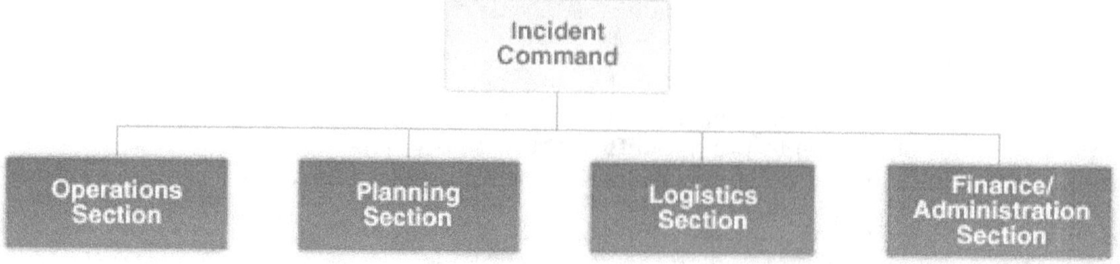

The General Staff, or Section Chiefs, report directly to the Incident Commander.

General Staff Overview

The General Staff overall responsibilities at an incident scene are summarized below:

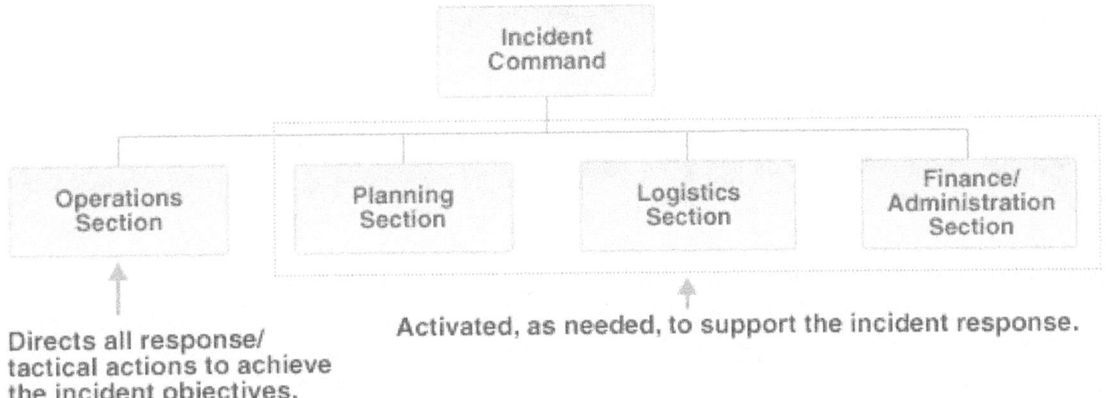

In an expanding incident, the Incident Commander first establishes the Operations Section. The remaining Sections are established as needed to support the operation.

ICS Position Titles: Review

ICS supervisory titles are important because they allow many different agencies to work together under a common organizational structure. Using consistent titles ensures that personnel from different organizations have the same credentials and qualifications. Let's review the ICS supervisory titles:

Organizational Level	Title	Support Position
Incident Command	Incident Commander	Deputy
Command Staff	Officer	Assistant
General Staff (Section)	Chief	Deputy
Branch	Director	Deputy
Division/Group	Supervisor	N/A
Unit	Leader	Manager
Strike Team/Task Force	Leader	Single Resource Boss

ICS Organizational Components

Section: The organizational level with responsibility for a major functional area of incident management (e.g., Operations, Planning, Logistics, Finance/Administration). The person in charge of each Section is designated as a Chief.

Division: The organizational level having responsibility for operations within a defined geographic area. The person in charge of each Division is designated as a Supervisor.

Group: An organizational subdivision established to divide the incident management structure into functional areas of operation. The person in charge of each Group is designated as a Supervisor.

Branch: An organizational level used when the number of Divisions or Groups exceeds the span of control. Can be either geographical or functional. The person in charge of each Branch is designated as a Director.

Task Force: A combination of mixed resources with common communications operating under the direct supervision of a Task Force Leader.

Strike Team: A set number of resources of the same kind and type with common communications operating under the direct supervision of a Strike Team Leader.

Single Resource: An individual, a piece of equipment and its personnel complement, or a crew or team of individuals with an identified supervisor that can be used at an incident.

Section Chiefs and Deputies

As mentioned previously, the person in charge of each Section is designated as a Chief. Section Chiefs have the ability to expand their Sections to meet the needs of the situation.

Each of the Section Chiefs may have a Deputy, or more than one, if necessary. The Deputy:

- May assume responsibility for a specific portion of the primary position, work as relief, or be assigned other tasks.
- Should always be as proficient as the person for whom he or she works.

When an incident involves multiple agencies, assigning Deputies from other organizations can increase interagency coordination.

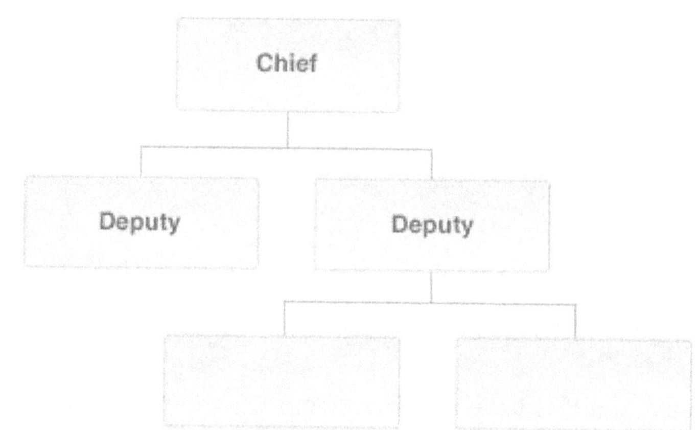

General Staff

As you previously learned, an Incident Commander is responsible for all incident management functions including: operations, planning, logistics, and finance and administration.

Depending on the incident needs, the Incident Commander may delegate some or all of these functions by establishing Sections. If a Section Chief is assigned to an incident, he or she will report directly to the Incident Commander.

Together, these Section Chiefs are referred to as the General Staff. Let's take a look at the responsibilities of each Section Chief.

The Operations Section Chief is responsible for developing and implementing strategy and tactics to accomplish the incident objectives. This means that the Operations Section Chief organizes, assigns, and supervises all the tactical or response resources assigned to the incident. Additionally, if a Staging Area is established, the Operations Section Chief would manage it.

The Planning Section Chief oversees the collection, evaluation, and dissemination of operational information related to the incident. It is the Planning Section's responsibility to prepare and disseminate the Incident Action Plan, as well as track the status of all incident resources.

The Planning Section helps ensure responders have accurate information and provides resources such as maps and floor plans.

The Logistics Section is responsible for providing facilities, services, and material support for the incident.

Logistics is critical on more complex incidents. The Logistics Section Chief assists the Incident Commander and Operations Section Chief by providing the resources and services required to support incident activities. During an incident, Logistics is responsible for ensuring the well-being of responders by providing sufficient food, water, and medical services. Logistics is also responsible for arranging communication equipment, computers, transportation, and anything else needed to support the incident.

Another critical function during complex incidents is Finance and Administration.

The Finance and Administration Section Chief is responsible for all of the financial and cost analysis aspects of an incident. These include contract negotiation, recording personnel and equipment time, documenting and processing claims for accidents and injuries occurring at the incident, and keeping a running tally of the costs associated with the incident.

We've now introduced you to the four ICS Sections.

It is important to remember that the ICS organizational structure is determined based on the incident objectives and resource requirements. It expands and contracts in a flexible manner. And, only those functions, positions, or sections necessary for a particular incident are filled.

Operations Section Chief

Typically, the Operations Section Chief is the person with the greatest tactical expertise in dealing with the problem at hand. The Operations Section Chief:

- Develops and implements strategy and tactics to carry out the incident objectives.
- Organizes, assigns, and supervises the tactical response resources.

Operations Section: Single Resources

Let's look at how resources are organized within the Operations Section. It all begins with Single Resources. Single Resources are individuals, a piece of equipment and its personnel complement, or a crew or team of individuals with an identified supervisor. On a smaller incident, the Operations Section may be comprised of an Operations Section Chief and single resources.

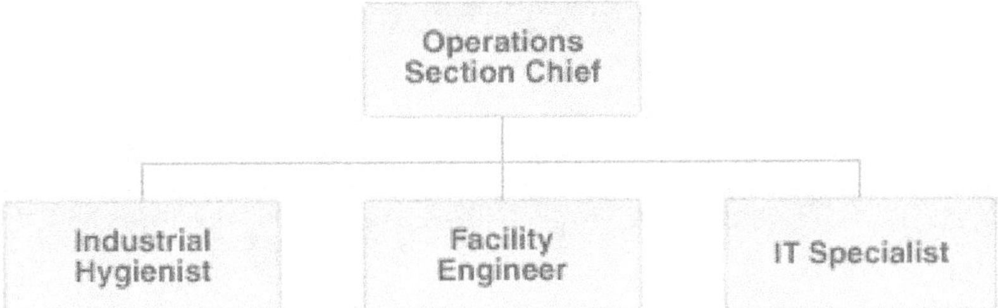

Operations Section: Teams

Single resources may be organized into teams. Using standard ICS terminology, the two types of team configurations are:

- **Task Forces** — A combination of **mixed resources** with common communications operating under the direct supervision of a Leader.
- **Strike Teams** — Consist of all **similar resources** with common communications operating under the direct supervision of a Leader.

Sample Strike Teams and Task Forces

The Operations Section organization chart shows possible team assignments in a flooding incident. Each team would have a Team Leader reporting to the Operations Section Chief.

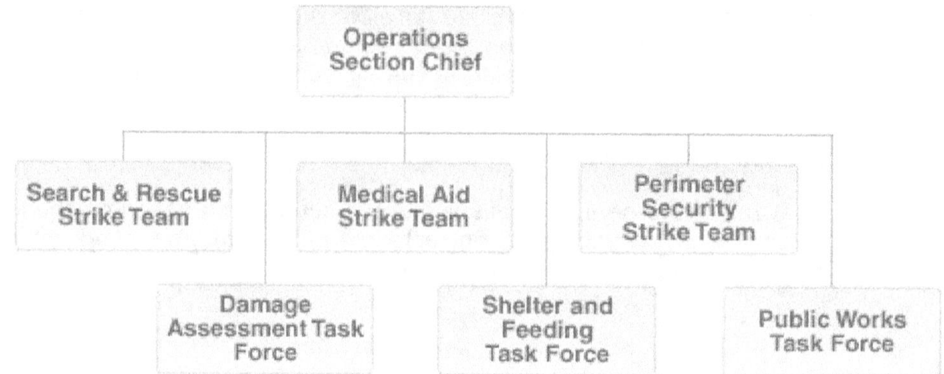

Note that these are examples of possible Strike Teams and Task Forces. These elements should be established based on the type of incident and unique requirements of the jurisdiction or agency.

Too Many Teams!

To maintain span of control, each team should be comprised of a Team Leader and no more than five to seven team members. As teams are added, what happens to the Operations Section Chief's span of control?

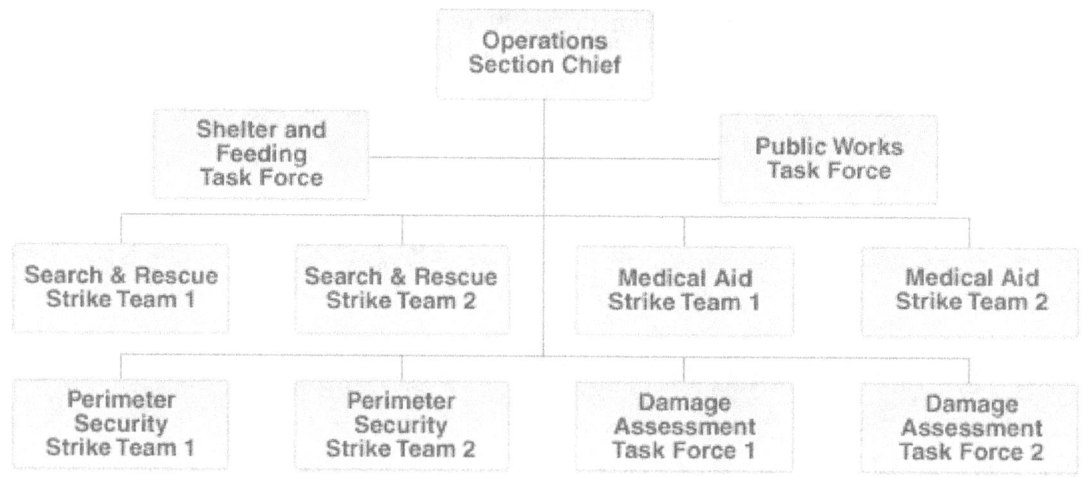

The Solution: Add Groups or Divisions

On a large, complex incident the Operations Section may become very large. Using the ICS principle of modular organization, the Operations Section may add the following elements to manage span of control:

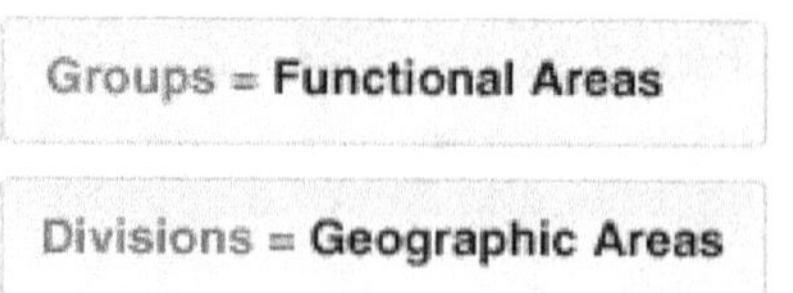

- **Groups** — Used to describe functional areas of operation.
- **Divisions** — Used to divide an incident geographically.

Maintaining Span of Control: Groups

The organization chart below illustrates how Groups can be used to maintain span of control within the Operations Section.

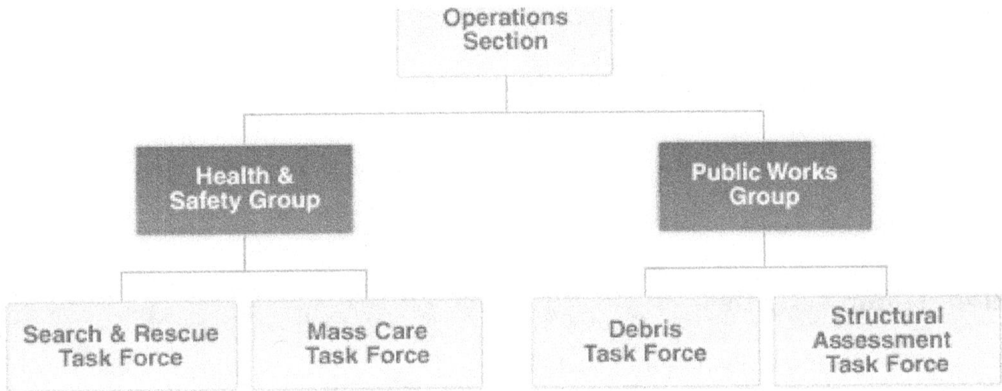

Maintaining Span of Control: Groups and Divisions (Geographic Areas)

The organization chart below illustrates how Groups and Divisions can be used together to maintain span of control within the Operations Section. The use of Divisions would be effective if the incident covered a large or isolated area of the community.

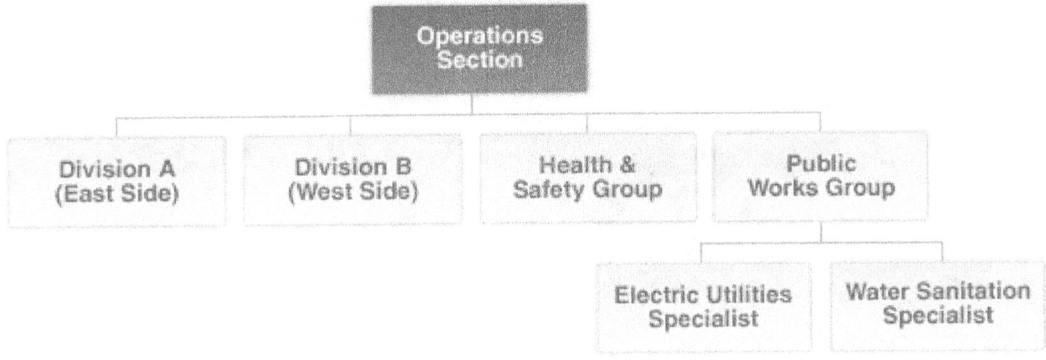

Operations Section: Establishing Branches

The Operations Section Chief may add Branches to supervise Groups and Divisions and further reduce his or her span of control.

The person in charge of each Branch is designated as a **Director**.

Review the chart. What are the advantages of reducing the Operations Section Chief's span of control?

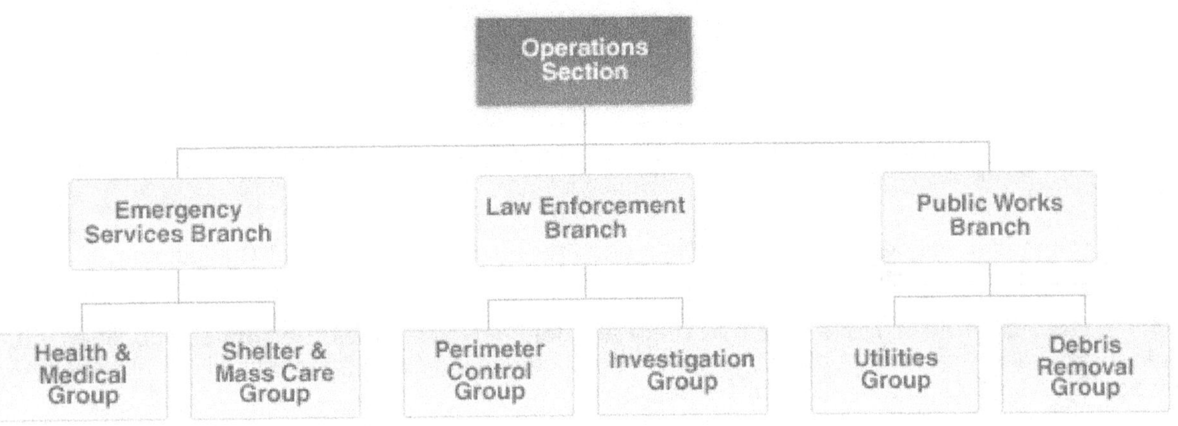

Planning Section

The Incident Commander will determine if there is a need for a Planning Section and, if so, will designate a Planning Section Chief.

If no Planning Section is established, the Incident Commander will perform all planning functions. It is up to the Planning Section Chief to activate any needed additional staffing.

Planning Section: Major Activities

The major activities of the Planning Section may include:

- Collecting, evaluating, and displaying incident intelligence and information.
- Preparing and documenting Incident Action Plans.
- Tracking resources assigned to the incident.
- Maintaining incident documentation.
- Developing plans for demobilization.

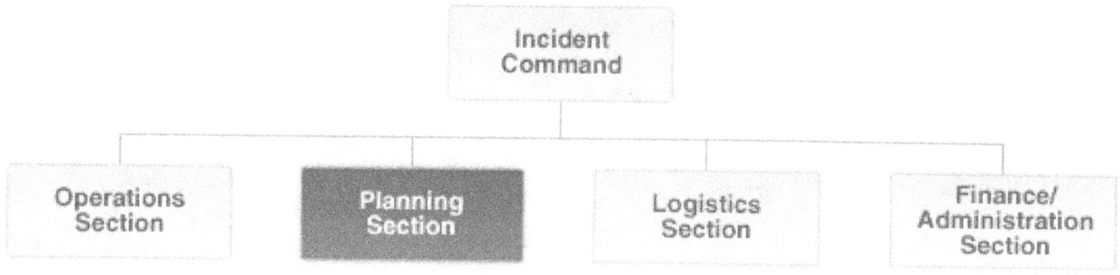

Planning Section Units

The Planning Section may include the following units:

Resources Unit: Responsible for recording the status of resources committed to the incident. This Unit also evaluates resources committed currently to the incident, the effects additional responding resources will have on the incident, and anticipated resource needs.

Situation Unit: Responsible for the collection, organization, and analysis of incident status information, and for analysis of the situation as it progresses.

Demobilization Unit: Responsible for ensuring orderly, safe, and efficient demobilization of incident resources.

Documentation Unit: Responsible for collecting, recording, and safeguarding all documents relevant to the incident.

Logistics Section

The Incident Commander will determine if there is a need for a Logistics Section at the incident, and if so, will designate an individual to fill the position of the Logistics Section Chief.

The Logistic Section Chief helps make sure that there are adequate resources (personnel, supplies, and equipment) for meeting the incident objectives. The Logistics Section Chief maintains his or her span of control by adding Branch Directors and Unit Leaders.

Logistics Section: Major Activities

The Logistics Section is responsible for all services and support needs, including:

- Ordering, obtaining, maintaining, and accounting for essential personnel, equipment, and supplies.
- Providing communication planning and resources.
- Setting up food services for responders.
- Setting up and maintaining incident facilities.
- Providing support transportation.
- Providing medical services to **incident personnel**.

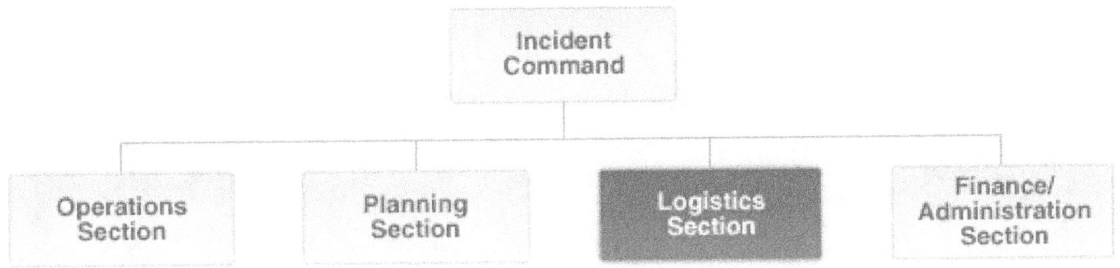

Logistics Section Units

Within the Logistics Section, the following six primary Units may be established:

Supply Unit: Orders, receives, stores, and processes all incident-related resources, personnel, and supplies.

Ground Support Unit: Provides all ground transportation during an incident. In conjunction with providing transportation, the Unit is also responsible for maintaining and supplying vehicles, keeping usage records, and developing incident Traffic Plans.

Facilities Unit: Sets up, maintains, and demobilizes all facilities used in support of incident operations. The Unit also provides facility maintenance and security services required to support incident operations.

Food Unit: Determines food and water requirements, plans menus, orders food, provides cooking facilities, cooks, serves, maintains food service areas, and manages food security and safety concerns.

Communications Unit: Major responsibilities include effective communications planning as well as acquiring, setting up, maintaining, and accounting for communications equipment.

Medical Unit: Responsible for the effective and efficient provision of medical services to incident personnel.

Finance/Administration Section

The Incident Commander will determine if there is a need for a Finance/Administration Section at the incident, and if so, will designate an individual to fill the position of the Finance/Administration Section Chief.

The Time, Compensation/Claims, Cost, and Procurement Units may be established within this Section.

Finance/Administration Section: Major Activities

The Finance/Administration Section is set up for any incident that requires incident-specific financial management. The Finance/Administration Section is responsible for:

- Contract negotiation and monitoring.
- Timekeeping.
- Cost analysis.
- Compensation for injury or damage to property.
- Documentation for reimbursement (e.g., under mutual aid agreements and assistance agreements).

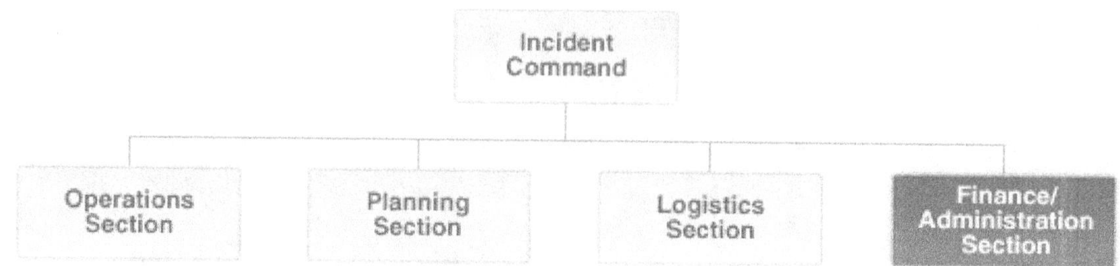

Finance/Administration Section Units

Within the Finance/Administration Section, the following four Units may be established:

Compensation/Claims Unit: Responsible for financial concerns resulting from property damage, injuries, or fatalities at the incident.

Cost Unit: Responsible for tracking costs, analyzing cost data, making estimates, and recommending cost savings measures.

Procurement Unit: Responsible for financial matters concerning vendor contracts.

Time Unit: Responsible for recording time for incident personnel and hired equipment.

Lesson Summary

This lesson introduced you to the General Staff, including:

- Roles and responsibilities.
- Position titles.

The next lesson focuses on how incidents are managed using Unified Command principles.

Lesson 5: Unified Command

Lesson Overview

The previous lessons covered Incident Command System (ICS) fundamentals. This lesson introduces you to the concepts of Unified Command and coordination.

By the end of this lesson, you should be able to:

- Define Unified Command.
- List the advantages of Unified Command.
- Differentiate between command and coordination.

Unified Command

The Unified Command organization consists of the Incident Commanders from the various jurisdictions or agencies operating together to form a single command structure in the field.

Unified Command Benefits

In a Unified Command, institutions and responding agencies blend into an integrated, unified team. A unified approach results in:

- A shared understanding of priorities and restrictions.
- A single set of incident objectives.
- Collaborative strategies.
- Improved internal and external information flow.
- Less duplication of efforts.
- Better resource utilization.

Incident Commanders Work Together

When implemented properly, Unified Command enables agencies with different legal, geographic, and functional responsibilities to coordinate, plan, and interact effectively.

The Incident Commanders within the Unified Command make joint decisions and speak as one voice. Any differences are worked out within the Unified Command.

Unity of command is maintained within the Operations Section. Each responder reports to a single supervisor within his or her area of expertise. Within a Unified Command, a police officer would not tell the firefighters how to do their job nor would the police direct search and rescue tactics.

Unified Command and NIMS

NIMS encourages the use of Unified Command.

"As a team effort, Unified Command allows all agencies with jurisdictional authority or functional responsibility for the incident to jointly provide management direction through a common set of incident objectives and strategies and a single Incident Action Plan. **Each participating agency maintains its authority, responsibility, and accountability.**"

Unified Command Features

Co-located (Shared) Facilities

In a Unified Command, incident facilities are co-located or shared.

Bringing the responsible officials, Command Staffs, and planning elements together in a single Incident Command Post can promote coordination.

Single Planning Process and Incident Action Plan

Unified Command uses a single planning process and produces one Incident Action Plan. The planning process for Unified Command is similar to the process used on single-jurisdiction incidents.

Integrated General Staff

Integrating multijurisdictional and/or multiagency personnel into various other functional areas may be beneficial. For example:

- In Operations and Planning, Deputy Section Chiefs can be designated from an adjacent jurisdiction.
- In Logistics, a Deputy Logistics Section Chief from another agency or jurisdiction can help to coordinate incident support.

Incident Commanders within the Unified Command must concur on the selection of the General Staff Section Chiefs. The Operations Section Chief must have full authority to implement the tactics within the Incident Action Plan.

Coordinated Process for Resource Ordering

The Incident Commanders within the Unified Command work together to establish resource ordering procedures that allow for:

- Deployment of scarce resources to meet high-priority objectives.
- Potential cost savings through agreements on cost sharing for essential services.

Possible Unified Command Organization

Below is a possible Unified Command organizational structure for a hazardous materials incident.

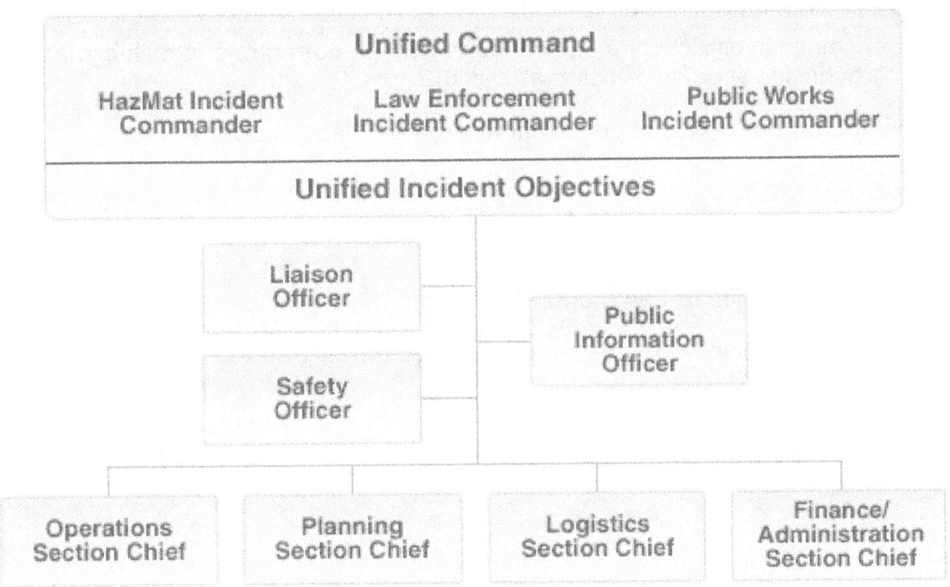

Incident Coordination

Coordination includes the activities that ensure that the onsite ICS organization receives the information, resources, and support needed to achieve the incident objectives. Coordination takes place in a number of entities and at all levels of government. Examples of coordination activities include:

- Establishing policy based on interactions with agency executives, other agencies, and stakeholders.
- Collecting, analyzing, and disseminating information to support the establishment of a common operating picture.
- Establishing priorities among incidents.
- Resolving critical resource issues.
- Facilitating logistics support and resource tracking.
- Synchronizing public information messages to ensure everyone is speaking with one voice.

Emergency Operations Center Role

Typically, an Emergency Operations Center (EOC) supports the on-scene response by relieving the Incident Commander of the burden of external coordination and securing additional resources.

An EOC is:

- A physical location.
- Staffed with personnel trained for and authorized to represent their agency/discipline.
- Equipped with mechanisms for communicating with the incident site and obtaining resources and potential resources.
- Managed through protocols.
- Applicable at different levels of government.

EOCs may be established at the Federal, State, tribal, and local levels.

Joint Information Center

Another coordination entity is the Joint Information Center (JIC). The JIC:

- May be established to coordinate all incident-related public information activities.
- Serves as the central point of contact for all news media. When possible, public information officials from all participating agencies should co-locate at the JIC.

JICs may be established at various levels of government or at incident sites.

Lesson Summary

This lesson familiarized you with Unified Command and coordination principles. Remember that:

- Unified Command enables agencies with different legal, geographic, and functional responsibilities to coordinate, plan, and interact effectively.
- Coordination provides strategic and policy guidance, information, and resource support, while the incident command structure in the field retains control of the incident operations and keeps policymakers and the EOC informed.

www.ingramcontent.com/pod-product-compliance
Lightning Source LLC
Chambersburg PA
CBHW080903260726
48660CB00009B/3421